· LOCAL · FLAVOUR · SERIES ·

COOKING
&
LOOKING
in
FREMANTLE

Compiled and
illustrated by
·Rosemary·
·Sinclair·

Edited by
·Joy·
·Hayes·

AYERS & JAMES HERITAGE BOOKS
Sydney 1985

Titles available in the
Local Flavour Series:

Cooking & Looking in Canberra
Cooking & Looking in Sydney's Rocks Area
Cooking & Looking in Cairns & District
Cooking & Looking in Fremantle

© Rosemary Sinclair, 1986

All rights reserved. No part of this publication may be reproduced, stored in a retrieval system, or transmitted in any form or by any means, electronic, mechanical, photocopying, recording, or otherwise, without prior permission of the author.

Illustrated by Rosemary Sinclair
Designed by Judy Hungerford
Project editing by Joy Hayes, Creative Pages
Project management by Book Production Services Pty Ltd
Typeset and assembled by Rochester Photosetting Service
Printed in Singapore
ISBN 0 949256 07 2

C·O·N·T·E·N·T·S

On Measurements 4

*

INTRODUCTION 7

*

OLD TIMERS 11

*

RESTAURANTS & TEA ROOMS 25

*

POPULAR PUBS 47

*

ARTS & CRAFTS 65

*

FREMANTLE FOLK 79

*

Recipe Index 95

ON MEASUREMENTS

Trying new recipes has long been one of my favourite pastimes, and because the major difficulty encountered has been working out stipulated measurements, I've tried to make the recipes easy for everybody to follow.

Keeping in mind that cooking is an art, *not* a science, I've used cup measurements where practicable (i.e. ordinary tea-cup size not the little dainty one!). Otherwise, measurements are given in both the metric and imperial scales.

Some cooks believe it necessary to weigh everything, but I've never done so, and can't recall any failures as a result.

GENERAL MEASUREMENTS
FOR SCALE-SCORNING COOKS

1 cup liquid	250 ml	= (½ pt)
2 cups solid butter	500 g	= (1 lb)
2 cups granulated sugar	500 g	= (1 lb)
2½ cups icing sugar	500 g	= (1 lb)
1 level tablespoon butter	15 g	= (½ oz)
2 level tablespoons flour	10 g	= (¼ oz)
1 tablespoon	20 ml	
1 teaspoon	5 ml	

Note: Approximate North American measurements appear in brackets. North American readers should also note that their tablespoon equals 15 ml or 3 teaspoons.

OVEN TEMPERATURES

It is difficult to advise exact oven temperatures as different makes of stoves give different results at the same temperature reading. Indeed, many fuel stoves still in use have no temperature gauge, and a degree of guesswork is unavoidable.

The following chart should be helpful for most stoves.

OVEN DESCRIPTION	TEMPERATURE GAUGE		
	Automatic Electric	*Gas*	*0°C (or Celsius)*
Cool	200	200	100
Very slow	250	250	120
Slow	300–325	300	150–160
Moderately slow	325–350	325	160–170
Moderate	350–375	350	170–190
Moderately hot	375–400	375	190–200
Hot	400–450	400	200–230
Very hot	450–500	450	230–260

Today let to employees of
Fremantle Prison, these quaint
terraced cottages were built by
convicts to house Pensioner
Guards and their families.

I·N·T·R·O·D·U·C·T·I·O·N

A few days in Fremantle is not enough. A city steeped in history, alive with culture, exuding the warmth of a small community of multicultural character, it deserves more than a cursory glance. The rewards are plentiful.

Until recently my own impressions of Fremantle resulted from a flick-of-the-eye visit in the early 1960s.

In recent years my interest in the place was thoroughly awakened during a long look with a local resident. Excited, I itched to delve into its history, to talk with people whose ancestors settled the place, to look behind the beautiful building facades, to absorb the culture evident in the countless craft and art establishments. I wanted to wander along the waterfront and wonder at the resourcefulness of the early fishermen who established the thriving fishing industry, to ponder the plight of convicts — thousands of them — brought here from 1850 to build the colony. They were all minor offence men who first had to build their own prison, a twelve-sided slice of history called 'the Round House'.

Its discovery by Captain James Stirling on HMS *Success* in 1827 led to Fremantle's establishment as a British settlement in 1829 when Captain Charles Howe Fremantle sailed HMS *Challenger* to the west coast.

The first settlers arrived on the *Parmelia* in June 1829 and soon after the colony of Western Australia was proclaimed. The capital, Perth, was founded in August the same year.

Fremantle from the early days of the colony was a busy port and according to John and Ray Oldham in their book *Western Heritage* it was 'an untidy place with little plan and no unity. The most prominent building from sea or land had been the Round House, the old gaol on Arthur's Head. Roads were little better than sandy tracks and sand permeated everywhere'.

It changed dramatically in the 1850s with many notable buildings being erected along with good roads, jetties and wharves. Much of the work was carried out by convict labour brought out for the purpose.

Then the discovery of gold in the 1890s in Coolgardie and Kalgoorlie put Fremantle well and truly on the map! It became a hive of industry with an enormous population increase. It wasn't long before Fremantle became a modern maritime city and the chief port of call in Western Australia.

One of Fremantle's greatest attractions is the friendliness of its people. Warm and welcoming, they generally exude a cheery attitude so rare in a busy world. Their contributions and offers of assistance in the preparation of this book were so overwhelming that my greatest difficulty was condensing and cutting!

Places which have not, by reasons of space requirements, been given detailed inclusion within these pages but are worthy of mention and a close inspection include the Oriental Family Hotel, the Fremantle Gaol and Museum, the Maritime Museum, Bateman's Hardware Store, all other churches, the P&O Building, Elder Building, Philimore Chambers, Princess May Girls' School, the Film and Television Institute, Cicerello's Fish Markets — just to mention a few.

Outside the city centre the suburbs provide an exciting variety of splendid buildings, some of such charming character they prompt 'oohs' and 'aahs' and lingering looks.

So many enchanting private dwellings I wanted to draw, but sadly time and space would not allow such indulgence. Visitors would be well rewarded with a suburban tour.

It is not surprising that Fremantle in 1983 won the International Tourist Award for Heritage — with official recognition for being the most complete nineteenth century port city in the world.

In 1986, with feverish improvements in preparation for an expected influx of visitors to this America's Cup venue, Fremantle must surely rank as one of the world's most exciting and charming port cities.

For their assistance in the preparation of this book thanks go to Cynthia Anthony (Fremantle City Library), Robyn Baylis, Marjorie Baguley, Brenda Blackstock, Eileen Bond, Bread and Cheese Shop, Cafe 33, Joan Campbell (Potters Workshop), Captain Fremantle Motor Lodge, Elizabeth Chapin (Lauder and Howard), Coufie's Cafe, Culley's Tea Rooms, Justin Cunningham, John A

Cutting (Fremantle Chamber of Commerce), Enrico D'Alessandro, Dawn Davies (Oyster Beds Restaurant), Esplanade Hotel, Federal Hotel, Fremantle Arts Centre, the *Fremantle Gazette*, Fremantle Hotel, John Gordon (Bannister Street Craftworks), Harper and Whittingtons (Fremantle Markets), The Health Hut, Val Heaney, Penny Holmes, Michael Kailis, Agnisha Kera (Fremantle City Council), Les Lauder, Lido Restaurant, Lombardo's Fisherman's Landing, Magic Apple, Mason's Brasserie (Sail and Anchor Hotel), Enid Maxted, Mexican Kitchen, Suzie Money (Sales Executive, Esplanade Hotel), Christine Morgan (Fremantle Markets Coffee Shop), National Hotel, Norfolk Hotel, Papa Luigi's, Mr Pickwick's Gourmet Delicatessen, Pioneer Cafe, Princess Coffee Lounge, Murray Rann (Fremantle Port Authority), Roma Restaurant, Roger Salis (Executive Chef, Esplanade Hotel), Timothy's Toys and Cicerello's.

With special thanks for assistance far beyond expectation to Dorothy Connolly, Dr Patricia Kailis (M. G. Kailis Group of Companies), Mr and Mrs Bruce Lee, Jan Oldham, Ray Oldham, Larraine Stevens (Fremantle City Council Library), Jim Stitt and Lucy Stitt.

Proclamation Tree

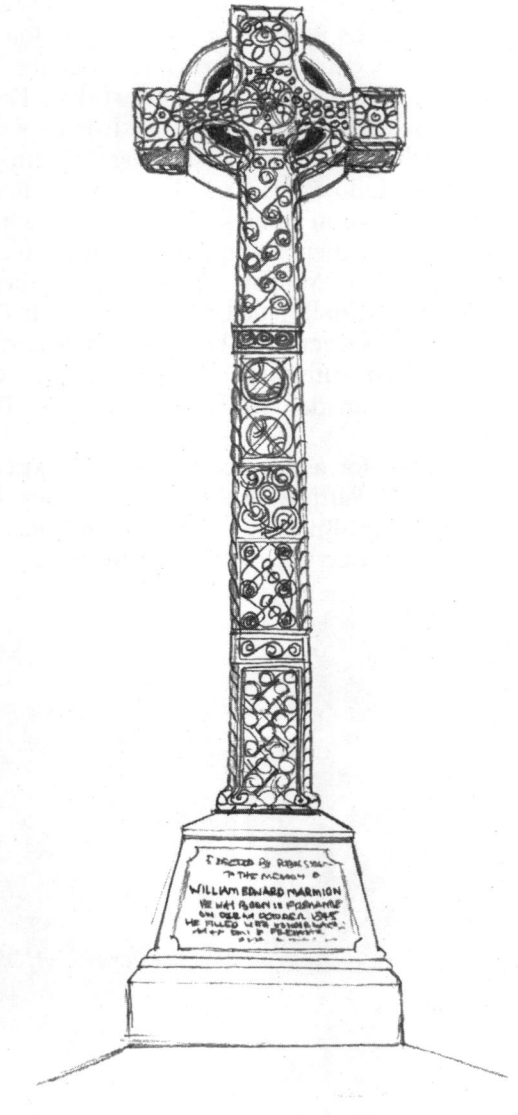

This intricately designed Marmion Memorial in the form of a Saxon Cross is situated close by the Proclamation Tree.

* O·L·D T·I·M·E·R·S *

In this section I have told the story of some of Fremantle's oldest buildings and have included some recipes for dishes that the early settlers of this fascinating city may have partaken.

SUFFOLK MARYS

Mix together:
60 g (2 oz) grated cheese
60 g (2 oz) plain flour sifted with *1 heaped teaspoon baking powder*
½ teaspoon dry mustard
60 g (2 oz) mashed potatoes
salt and *pepper*
½ of 1 beaten egg

Roll out, using more flour if mixture breaks. Cut into rounds, brush with *beaten egg* and bake in a very hot oven 230°C (450°F) until risen and well browned.

Split open, insert a large dab of *butter* and serve hot.

CWA Cookery Book (WA), 1936

STOVIES
(A Favourite Old Dish)

Slice up *potatoes* and *onions*, enough to fill frying pan. Season lightly with *salt* and *pepper* and put rashers of *bacon* on top, barely cover with *water* and put a large plate or lid on top. Steam slowly on the side of stove. Very tasty.

CWA Cookery Book (WA), 1936

THE ROUND HOUSE

One of Western Australia's most famous buildings, it actually has twelve equal sides! Despite this, it has always been known as the Round House.

Planned for use as a gaol, building began in September 1830 and was completed in January 1831. It was one of the first buildings in Fremantle and was the Swan River settlement's first important public construction.

Records reveal that 'a tiny hamlet clustered below this gaol, with sandhills and scrubby bush and scores of grasstrees or "blackboys"'.

Building materials came from the site and the contractor/builder, Richard Lewis, was instructed to finish it 'in a masterly manner'. The gaol contained eight cells and sometimes fifteen prisoners were squashed into each! The original weatherboard roof soon had to be better waterproofed with shingles. (Early settlers found, by trial and error, that she-oak, cut with the grain, was the best timber for roof shingles.)

The building's architect was Henry Revely, the colony's first civil engineer. He had joined Governor James Stirling's pioneer transport *Parmelia* at Cape Town. The Round House was most probably Revely's first major assignment.

A stone well in the middle supplied the guards and inmates with their water — it had been sunk down through the limestone and its construction must have been extremely difficult. The well has since been filled in.

Bread for the guards and prisoners was baked in an oven built into the stone steps and from this very spot a fifteen-year-old convict was hanged for murder!

During the convict period (1850–68) the Round House always had 'full house'. In those days a bell was rung in Fremantle's streets at 9.50 pm and anybody found outside after 10 pm was automatically bundled into the Round House lock-up, unless he or she could prove their free status.

Below the Round House there still exists a whalers' tunnel, constructed under Arthur Head as a direct route to the old shipping jetty and the Fremantle Whaling Company's stores and boats.

AUNTY ALICE'S ORANGE BAR CAKE

Aunty to everybody, Alice Gerrard lived for 26 years (until early 1986) in a cottage near the Round House. For many years she worked in the Harbour Trust canteen.

In the bowl of an electric mixer put:
2 cups self-raising flour
1 cup sugar
1 tablespoon grated orange rind
2 egg yolks
⅔ cup milk
250 g (8 oz) butter, roughly chopped

Beat on medium speed for 4 minutes. Divide between two greased bar tins.

Bake in a moderate oven 180°C (350°F) for 40–45 minutes until done when tested.

Turn out onto a wire rack and, when cold, ice with *orange icing*.

KANGAROO TAIL & PIG'S HEAD BRAWN

Put in a large saucepan:
1 *kangaroo tail*, cut or jointed
½ *small pig's head*
1 *blade mace*
1 *dessertspoon mixed herbs*
salt and *pepper*

Boil until meat falls off the bone (a few hours) then take out all the bones and pour the mixture into shallow dishes and let stand until set. It needs cool weather or an ice chest.

CWA Cookery Book (WA), 1936

Ships Supplied
William Pearce, Butcher, begs leave to inform Captains and Owners of Ships that he will supply them with good fresh Beef or Mutton, Livestock, Vegetables, etc., on the most reasonable terms, and at the shortest notice.

The Inquirer, 3 December 1851

HOME-MADE BREAD

Marjorie Baguley, a longtime resident of Fremantle, claims that this recipe gives excellent results.

Combine in a small bowl or saucepan:
3 *teaspoons dry yeast*
1 *teaspoon sugar*
2 *cups warm water* (not hot!)

Set aside in a warm place until frothy — 15–20 minutes.

In a large bowl put:
1⅛ *kg (2¼ lb) plain flour*, sifted
¼ *cup sugar*
1 *teaspoon salt*
½ *cup safflower or peanut oil*
1½ *cups warm water*

Mix to a dough, cover with a cloth and leave in a warm place to rise. When doubled in bulk turn out onto a floured bench and knead again. Divide into loaves and put in greased loaf tins.

When doubled in volume, bake at 190°C (375°F) for about 40 minutes.

A Visitor's View of Fremantle
Nearly blinded with dust or sand I eventually arrived in the main street. It is not so wide as King William Street, Adelaide, but it is long and has footpaths on both sides, though passengers walk in the middle of the road for reasons unknown.

Everything is white — roads, footpaths and houses, which with a tropical sun playing on them causes a glare, calculated to blind any ordinary being and makes the use of smoked glass absolutely necessary.

The Inquirer and Commercial News, 4 January 1888

BREAD AND BUTTER PUDDING

Cut *2 slices buttered bread* into fingers.

Beat *2 eggs* with *1 tablespoon sugar* then add *1 generous cup of milk*.

Place the bread in a small pie dish and pour the eggs and milk over.

Sprinkle with *grated nutmeg*.

Stand in an ovenproof dish of cold *water* and bake in a moderate oven until set — about 40 minutes.

A handful of *currants* or *sultanas* may be sprinkled among the pieces of bread if desired.

Serve chilled.

FREMANTLE TOWN HALL

The laying of the foundation stone for Fremantle's Town Hall took place in September 1885 and a banquet was held at the Oddfellows Hall to celebrate the occasion. Special guests at the function included the Governor of Western Australia and the Lord Mayor of Perth.

Recommendations by the Fremantle Town Trust (the forerunner of the Fremantle Municipal Council), put to and approved by the State Governor, included the use of prison labour to construct the new building from stone supplied from the government quarry at North Fremantle.

The Town Hall was completed in 1887 at a cost of £14,000. The triangular shaped building featured a clock tower with a portico beneath. According to a visiting journalist at the time its 'elegance and appearance is equal to similar buildings in Victoria'.

Commenting on the building following its official opening in June 1887 the *West Australian* said:

> The new Town Hall lends itself admirably to . . . festivities, ample space being available . . . in the numerous departments which surround the tessellated open triangle in the centre of the building.

Over the years the Town Hall has had numerous renovations and facelifts. Expenditure approved by the Fremantle Council in 1976 for updating the acoustics has improved the building's effectiveness as a modern-day public meeting place.

Today the Town Hall stands as one of Fremantle's most attractive buildings.

The First Dance
With respect to the dance floor, we might say that considering that it was in use for the first time, it was in splendid condition and experienced devotees of the Terpsichorean art had no difficulty in indulging in their favourite pastime.

The Weekly Times, 25 June 1887

OLD TIMERS * 18

Unveiled in 1911, this bronze statue stands as a tribute to C.Y. O'Connor. A great engineer, he is also credited with providing inland Kalgoorlie with fresh water pumped 556 kilometres from Perth.

C. Y. O'Connor

Charles Yelverton O'Connor is the man credited with designing and building Fremantle Harbour. After his appointment in 1891 as Engineer-in-Chief for Western Australia, he overcame much opposition to have his plans accepted.

The first British Royal Mail Steamer to call at the Port of Fremantle was the *Himalaya* in 1901 — captained by Commander Brown, a native of Fremantle.

During celebrations to mark the importance of the occasion (presided over by the State Premier, Sir John Forrest), C. Y. O'Connor reminded those gathered that in November 1892 he had undertaken to have the Harbour sufficiently advanced by the end of eight years so as to permit the entrance of the largest steamers. The undertaking was fulfilled well within time.

While work was far from completed at the time of his death in 1902, it was so well planned that its anchorage had contributed greatly to the prosperity of Western Australia.

Descendants of C. Y. O'Connor have also made their mark. Two of his great-grandsons, brothers Jeremy and John Dawkins, currently hold important public positions. Jeremy is a town planner for the city of Fremantle and John is a member of parliament representing the federal electorate of Fremantle.

RABBIT PASTE

Cut *1 rabbit* into joints, put in a saucepan with *1 blade of mace* and *2 tablespoons water* and simmer gently for 1 hour. Add *2 rashers bacon*, derinded and diced, cook 10 minutes and add *½ cup water*. Simmer another hour.

Pour gravy into a cup.

Separate the meat from the bones and put through a mincer. Add *pepper* and *salt* to taste then add the gravy and a little *grated nutmeg*.

Mix well and put into small jars with *melted butter* on top. This is very nice for school lunches.

CWA Cookery Book (WA), 1936

FREMANTLE RAILWAY STATION

In 1905 a decision was taken to erect a new station at Market Street to replace two former railway stations, one built in 1880, opposite Mouat Street, the second in 1887 in Cliff Street. The latter structure was built purely to provide employment for a great number of men without jobs. It was described in the local press, as 'sufficient proof that ideas formally entertained of what was required for railway accommodation arose from inexperience in these matters and a want of knowledge of the "iron horse"'.

Designed by Mr Dartnell, Chief Engineer of Existing Lines, the Market Street station's builder was S. B. Alexander who completed his portion of the works within ten months. The Railway Department had previously constructed the foundations for the building.

When opened on 1 July 1907, the station, with its parkland surrounds, was noted as having 'a very pleasing appearance, especially at night when the numerous lamps are lighted'.

The massive appearance of the facade belies the large span beyond — a feature of many nineteenth century European stations. The building is constructed mostly in Donnybrook stone.

The station consists of three platforms connected by a subway 4.5 metres wide. A subway and electric lifts are used for movement of luggage and goods from one platform to another.

Business in Fremantle was significantly altered by the siting of the new railway station — a *Herald* article criticised the site selection, noting that the station was built at the 'very extremity of the town instead of as near to the centre as possible'.

Buses replaced the rail service between Fremantle and Perth in 1979. Suggestions were then put forward for the use of the station as a permanent residence for various community organisations — all were rejected.

In 1983 the station had a major facelift prior to the reintroduction of the rail service soon after.

Today the building is recognised as one of the port's most interesting architectural features and commuters enjoy a regular rail service to and from Perth.

Be Prepared

. . . the battle over public toilets still has not been resolved.

The public toilets will continue to be open only when the station is staffed, so if you travel on Sunday be prepared.

Fremantle Gazette, 14 March 1984

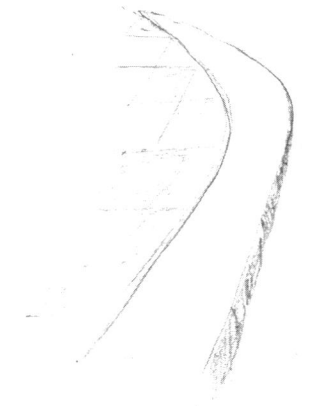

THE SAMSONS OF SAMSON HOUSE

Lionel Samson and his brother William came to Australia on the *Calista* just two months after Captain James Stirling arrived with the first settlers on the *Parmelia*.

The *Calista* was the second passenger vessel to arrive in the colony, and for Lionel Samson, formerly of the London Stock Exchange, the environment must have been quite a shock.

In 1829, the same year he landed in Fremantle, he set up business as a wine and spirit merchant, importer and auctioneer. (Lionel Samson (1829) Pty Ltd is Australia's oldest established family business.) His brother, William, stayed in the business for eighteen years before moving to Adelaide.

Lionel returned to England in 1842 and married Fanny Levi, daughter of the founder of the London Stock Exchange. They returned to live in Perth where they had three sons and three daughters.

Lionel Samson was a prominent figure in public and business life in Perth and Fremantle, and two of his sons became mayors of Fremantle.

When Lionel died in 1878 the business was carried on by his son Michael. It has continued in the family's control to this day.

Not surprisingly, the name Samson is synonymous with Fremantle. Several business houses carry the name, and Samson House — built for Michael Samson in 1888–89 — will be opened to the public in 1987. It was here Michael and his wife Mary reared three children, William Frederick (later Sir Frederick), Kathleen and Adelaide.

Sir Frederick Samson became a passionate advocate of Fremantle and is well recognised as one of the city's finest sons. In his younger days he studied engineering, joined the Air Force, worked for the Water Board and after World War I became a surveyor.

He established a real estate business in 1931 and in 1935 married Daphne Marks.

Sir Frederick was elected to Fremantle Council in 1936 and so began a 37-year career in local government — 21 of those years as mayor — a record term.

He retired in 1972 at the age of 80 and died in 1974.

According to Bruce Lee, who served with Sir Frederick on the Fremantle Council for many years, Sir Frederick was very fond of giving civic receptions. Mr Lee cannot recall a visit from a naval

vessel going without such an event. On these occasions, the mayor would invariably hand the guest of honour a cup of tea and say:

> I am conferring on you the Freedom of the City. In Fremantle, we honour the Loyal Toast in Tea, and since we have been doing that I am given to understand that Her Royal Highness has never been in better health.

At the conclusion of the speeches Sir Frederick would catch the eye of the Town Hall caretaker who acted as steward, and say, 'Mac, we'll sail around the Buoy'. This was the signal for the serving of liquor and soft drinks. Mayor Samson, himself a teetotaller, was an excellent host.

Sir Frederick is credited with playing a vital role in the restoration of the Round House. He was also instrumental in the establishment of the Fremantle Museum and Arts Centre, the Community Education Centre, and the Perth Institute of Film and Television.

No wonder he was affectionately known as 'Mr Fremantle'.

LUCY'S DATE LOAF

In a saucepan put:
250 g (8 oz) chopped dates
60 g (2 oz) butter
1 level teaspoon bicarbonate of soda
1 cup water
Boil 5 minutes (watch carefully as it may boil over very quickly)
Allow to cool and stir in:
1 beaten egg
1¾ cups self-raising flour
Turn into a greased loaf tin and bake in a moderate oven 180°C (350°F) for 45 minutes until cooked.

* R·E·S·T·A·U·R·A·N·T·S & T·E·A *
R·O·O·M·S

Here you'll find irresistible recipes from a cross-section of Fremantle's fine eating establishments.

SMOKED SALMON MOUSSE

A delicious entree from Captain Fremantle's restaurant within the Captain Fremantle Motor Lodge.

Blend:
200 g (6½ oz) cream cheese
2 tablespoons lemon juice
1 tablespoon horseradish
3 tablespoons finely diced onion
3 tablespoons chopped parsley
1 x 220 g can red salmon

Line 4 small terrine dishes with a slice of *smoked salmon* each, then spoon the blended mixture into the dishes level with the top. Turn the salmon overlap towards the centre of each dish and refrigerate for 12 hours.

Garnish with *sliced onion* and *capers*.

Serve with fresh *toasted bread*.

Serves 4.

CRAYFISH MARTINIQUE

Nothing but fresh crayfish is used in Fremantle and this recipe utilises them to perfection.

Remove the flesh from 4 *crayfish tails* and cut into 2.5 cm (1 in) medallions. Reserve the shells to use as dishes.

Make *white sauce*:
In a saucepan melt 1 *tablespoon butter*, off heat mix in 2 *tablespoons flour* then, over heat, add slowly 1 *cup milk*, stirring until smooth. Allow to cool.

Stir in:
½ *cup sour cream*
3 *tablespoons lemon juice*
1 *clove garlic*, crushed (or to taste)

Return to the heat, adding:
crayfish medallions
½ *cup sliced mushrooms*

Simmer 5 minutes then return the mixture to the crayfish shells.

Garnish with *lemon wedges* and *parsley*.

May be served with *rice*.

Serves 4.

An Ill Wind
A problem has been solved!!! The violent storm last week, resulted in the South Jetty, built 1856, becoming a beginning and an end, with no middle; it has washed away!!! The isolated cranes look most forlorn, but it is surely much better that a rotten structure, a week ago called a jetty, is now in ruin.

The Herald, 6 July 1872

MR PICKWICK'S GOURMET SHOP

One of many shops in the attractive Fremantle Malls, this was named after the Dickens character who was perhaps not a gourmet, but the title is in keeping with the old-world character of the Malls.

Mr Pickwick's began as a specialty food shop but now operates as a gourmet lunch bar. Special features include a hot carvery, extra special sandwich and roll fillings and a great selection of homemade lines. The following recipes are tempting samples.

PUMPKIN SOUP

In a large saucepan combine:
4 cups chicken stock
500 g (1 lb) pumpkin, peeled and chopped
3 large potatoes, peeled and chopped
1 large onion, peeled and finely chopped
½ teaspoon mixed herbs
½ teaspoon salt or to taste
pepper
Bring to boil and simmer until the vegetables are tender.

Puree in a blender or food processor and leave soup for at least 24 hours before serving, to develop the flavour.

The soup can be frozen until required.

Serves 6.

SAVOURY RISSOLES

In a bowl combine:
500 g (1 lb) minced steak
½ cup tomato sauce
1 cup breadcrumbs
1 egg, beaten
1 tablespoon mixed herbs
1 tablespoon chicken bouillon
1 cup grated carrot
1 onion, finely chopped
salt and pepper to taste

Form into round patties and cook in a heavy-based frypan with a little heated oil just covering the base.

Makes 8–10.

LOMBARDO'S

One of the best-known fishing families in Fremantle, the Lombardo family's association with the city began in 1926.

In that year, twelve-year-old Vincenzo Lombardo jumped ship at Busselton, was arrested and later released to the custody of a priest. By the early 1930s Vince Lombardo had taken up fishing and settled in Fremantle.

The fishing industry contributed greatly to Fremantle's survival when the importance of the port declined after the Second World War. The industry developed strongly and each year since 1948 the colourful Blessing of the Fleet ceremony has become a highlight of the city's cultural activities. There are many nationalities now involved in the fishing industry which provides for local and export markets.

During the Second World War, Vince Lombardo, like many of his recently migrated countrymen, was interned — leaving his wife to raise their children. He resumed fishing at the end of the war, and in 1947 he entered a joint venture with Roy Annear Senior (a descendant of Sam Annear, a convict guard on the first convict ship to reach the West's shores) to operate the *Penguin*, a lobster-fishing boat. This venture marked the beginning of the two families' joint involvement in several maritime ventures — culminating in Lombardo's Complex.

The Lombardo family is synonymous with the Fremantle fishing industry — all five sons have continued to work in businesses allied with the sea, and the family history is integrated with that of Fremantle.

In 1985 Vince Lombardo Senior was honoured with a special range of Hardy seafood wines in the series 'The Old Man and the Sea'.

This energetic and enterprising Fremantle family continues to make a positive contribution to the welfare of the city.

Lombardo's Complex on the waterfront contains restaurants, bars, function rooms, a nightclub and full service facilities for charter, private yachts and motor cruises.

The following recipes come from Lombardo's Fisherman's Landing.

YAKI TORI

This recipe comes from the Japanese restaurant within Lombardo's Fisherman's Landing complex.

Cut 215 g (7 oz) *chicken fillets* into cubes and thread onto bamboo skewers alternately with 2 *spring onions*, quartered and sectioned. Use 8 skewers in all.

Now prepare *Yaki Tori sauce*:
In a saucepan combine:
1 part soy sauce
1 part mirin sake
1 part sugar

Bring the sauce to boil, drop the skewers in and cook 10 minutes.

Remove and put under a heated griller for just a few minutes, dip into the sauce once more then give a final grill and they are ready to eat.

FISHERMAN'S PIE

Just one of the many delicious dishes served at the Fisherman's Landing — part of Lombardo's restaurant and entertainment complex.

First prepare *fish stock*:
In a saucepan put:
1 *fish head*
1 *onion*
1 *teaspoon mixed herbs*
1 *tablespoon chopped parsley*
1 *stalk celery*, chopped
1 *carrot*, chopped
salt and *pepper*
½ *cup white wine*
water to barely cover

Bring to the boil, boil about 15 minutes — no longer or it will become bitter. Strain and cool.

In a deep pan with a little *oil* and *butter*, saute until soft 1 *large onion*, chopped, and 1 *clove garlic*, finely chopped.

Add 1 *kg (2 lb) mixed fresh seafood* (e.g. prawns, squid, diced fish). Take off the heat and mix in 1 *tablespoon flour*, cook a little to make a roux, then add:
1 cup fish stock
1 *cup milk*
1 *bayleaf*
1 *tablespoon chopped parsley*

Stir until it boils but be careful not to overcook.

Transfer to a casserole.

Top with cooked *mashed potato* and *grated cheese* and bake in a hot oven, 220°C (430°F) until nicely brown.

This can also be topped with puff pastry or shortcrust.

Serve as is or with *rice*.

Serves 6.

COUFIE'S CAFE

This inviting building in East Fremantle's George Street presents a much happier image since its recent renovation. Previously run down and dilapidated, it reopened as a cafe early in 1986 under the ownership of Enrico D'Alessandro and three schoolteachers, one of whom is named Coufos — from which the name of the cafe was derived.

This specialty at Coufie's is made on the premises by Julie Wilson.

FETTUCCINE WITH CHEESE AND BACON SAUCE

Boil *185 g (6 oz) green fettuccine* until just soft, drain and run cold water over to prevent further cooking.

Make *cheese sauce*:
In a small saucepan melt *60 g (2 oz) butter* and stir in *2 tablespoons flour*. Cook without stirring until the mixture bubbles, remove from heat and stir in *1½ cups milk*. Bring to the boil, stirring constantly. Mix in *1 cup grated cheese*.

In a pan fry:
3 bacon rashers, derinded and chopped
1 large onion, chopped

In a shallow baking dish, place layers of fettuccine, cheese sauce, bacon and onion. Top with *1 cup grated cheese* and sprinkle with *paprika*.

Bake in hot oven 210°C (420°F) for 45 minutes.

Serve with a crisp *green salad*.

Serves 4.

Whalers
Between February 1837 and April 1837 no fewer than sixteen American Whalers called at Fremantle.
The Western Gateway
John K. Ewers

PIONEER CAFE

Operated by Margaret Collins and Marjorie Elliott since 1983, the Pioneer Cafe in the Fremantle Mall is open seven days a week.

Both English born, Margaret and Marjorie came to Australia in 1975, and worked at Myers in Fremantle before starting their business venture. They love the congenial, comfortable atmosphere and enjoy catering to the diverse groups who frequent the cafe. Here are three of their favourite recipes.

HAM AND EGG QUICHE

In a bowl put:
2 eggs
⅔ cup milk
Beat well and add *½ cup grated cheese* and a little *salt, pepper* and *nutmeg*.

Line a buttered flan or tart tin with *shortcrust pastry*, draping it over the tin to make it fit snugly against the sides without stretching it at all — if stretched it will shrink.

Trim the pastry edges holding the knife blade flat against the rim of the tin. (To prevent the pastry base becoming soggy or undercooked it is a good idea to bake the shell blind for 10–15 minutes before putting in the filling. Another idea is to place the quiche on a preheated baking sheet to cook.)

Arrange on the pastry *4–5 slices lean ham*, chopped, and gently pour over the egg mixture.

Bake in the middle of a hot oven 200°C (400°F) for 10 minutes, then lower the heat to 190°C (375°F) for a further 25 to 30 minutes until puffy and golden brown.

BEEF CURRY

In a large saucepan combine:
1 kg (2 lb) diced lean beef
1 large onion, chopped
1 medium carrot, diced
1 green apple, peeled and sliced
1 cup pineapple pieces

Bring to the boil and add:
1 tablespoon tomato paste
1 heaped tablespoon curry powder
2 teaspoons chili sauce or to taste
1 teaspoon tabasco or to taste

Cook gently until the meat is tender, and if a thicker consistency is desired, thicken with 1 dessertspoon cornflour mixed with ⅓ cup water.

Serve with fluffy rice.

Serves 6–8.

PIONEER CAFE SCONES

Into a bowl sift:
2½ cups self-raising flour
¼ teaspoon bicarbonate of soda
pinch salt

Rub in with the fingertips 45 g (1½ oz) butter until the texture resembles coarse breadcrumbs.

Add 1 cup buttermilk (or mixture of ½ cup milk and ½ cup cream) and mix lightly to a dough with a knife blade.

Turn the dough onto a floured board or workbench and roll to about 1 cm (½ in) thickness — this should be done quickly and with a light touch.

Cut the dough with a cutter into 5 cm (2 in) rounds, dust the tops with flour and put on a greased baking sheet.

Bake in a hot oven 230°C (450°F) for 15 minutes until puffed and golden brown.

Cool scones on a rack and eat while still warm.

ROMA RESTAURANT

One of the State's oldest restaurants, the Roma operated as a cafe before it was purchased by Frank Abrugiato in 1954. Today it is one of Fremantle's most popular, and locals have to share it with visitors from all over the world. It is very much a family business and Mrs Abrugiato and her daughter were in control on the day I visited.

A sign advertising 'ROAST CHICKEN TO TAKE AWAY, ONE POUND' is proudly displayed as the work of businessman Alan Bond — commissioned about thirty years ago during his less famous days as a signwriter.

CHICKEN AND SPAGHETTI

Place *whole chicken* on a greased baking dish or casserole and season with:
1 clove garlic, finely chopped
salt and *pepper*
2 teaspoons mixed herbs

Bake uncovered at 180°C (350°F) for 1½ hours.

Meanwhile, cook *310 g (10 oz)* best quality *pasta* in a pot of boiling *salted water* for 15 minutes, then drain, run cold water over and drain again.

Prepare *tomato sauce:*
In *a pan with a little butter* fry *3 large onions*, sliced, until soft but not brown.

Add:
1 clove garlic, finely chopped
1 small chili, seeded and finely chopped
a pinch of basil
salt and *pepper*

Cook gently for a few minutes, then stir in a *200 g (7 oz) can tomato paste*.

Add enough *chicken stock* to make about 3 cups sauce, and simmer for 45 minutes to 1 hour.

To serve, divide chicken into quarters. Arrange pasta on each plate alongside the chicken, pour tomato sauce over pasta and top with grated *parmesan cheese*.

Serves 4.

CAFE 33

The day I was there, this small pine-furnitured restaurant was choc-a-bloc with customers crowding the counter for tempting take-aways. Behind them, the cosy tables were all occupied. A large display board offered mouthwatering choices from rolls filled with pastrami, ham, pate or hoummus to vegetarian terrine or strudel.

Jennifer Coni and Raye Road enjoy the cafe business and do the cooking on the premises. Fremantle's attraction is its warm friendly atmosphere — for Jenny and Raye it is like a small country town and just as enjoyable.

Here are two favourites at Cafe 33.

SPINACH, NEW POTATO AND CHEESE SLICE

You'll need *one bunch* (about 10 large leaves) *silver beet*, minus stalks, and *10 small new potatoes*. Steam the silver beet until just wilted, drain and refresh under cold water. Squeeze out all the water and chop well.

Boil the whole potatoes until cooked, then dice.

In a large bowl combine:
the silver beet and potatoes
155 g (5 oz) crumbled fetta cheese
1 cup grated cheese (a mix of cheddar and sharp)
1 cup chopped spring onions
6 beaten eggs
salt and *lemon pepper* to taste
½ cup chopped parsley

Grease a baking dish (approximately 25 cm x 20 cm — 10 in x 8 in) with *butter* and gently pour the mixture into the dish.

Sprinkle with *extra grated cheese* and bake in a moderate oven ¾ to 1 hour, or until firm when touched.

Serve warm, cut into squares.

Serves 10–12.

FISH PATTIES

In a large bowl place:
1 x 425 g can tuna
1 cup frozen peas
1 x 375 g pkt instant mashed potato
1 cup grated cheese
1 cup grated carrot
1 cup chopped spring onions
1 cup chopped parsley
dash lemon pepper
dash salt
1 tablespoon softened butter
2 eggs

Mix thoroughly, pour on *boiling water* to make a workable mixture. It should not be too damp. Mix thoroughly again, shape into patties and roll in *flour*.

In a pan with hot *oil* just covering the base, cook on both sides until browned.

These can also be made into small balls and used for cocktail nibbles.

Makes about 15 patties.

Proclamation Day Sports, Fremantle Oval
A specially good running pig was emptied out of the bag, and gave the 8 or 9 competitors an excellent scamper from the start, beating the best of them. The grunter however, in its wisdom, doubled back on to the asphalt track where G. Phillimore found the tail, and the squealing porker was led off by his captor.

The Mail, 25 October 1904

SEAFOOD SALAD

One of Fremantle's oldest and best known restaurants, the Lido caters to lovers of Italian food.

In a large bowl combine:
1 medium sized calamari (squid) cleaned, cooked and diced
500 g (1 lb) mussels, cooked, shelled and diced
1 small crayfish, cooked and diced
215 g (7 oz) scallops, cooked and diced
1 can baby clams, drained
215 g (7 oz) prawns, shelled

Add and mix well:
1 green capsicum, seeded and sliced
1 red capsicum, seeded and sliced
2 sprigs parsley, chopped
1 medium sized white onion, sliced
2 tablespoons capers
3 baby gherkins, sliced
3 cloves garlic, finely chopped or crushed

Pour over dressing:
4 tablespoons olive oil
2 tablespoons vinegar   } combined
salt and *pepper* to taste
pinch chili powder

Serves 4.

Note: This may be stored for a week in the refrigerator by adding extra oil.

PAPA LUIGI'S

Papa Luigi's has been a favourite Fremantle spot for many years. Locals and tourists alike flock to taste its gelati, gourmet snacks and meals in the special atmosphere created with kerbside dining! Papa Luigi's, owned by Sicilian-born Nunzio Gumina, was the first cafe in Western Australia to serve its patrons at umbrellaed tables on the footpath — that first happened in 1979. In 1984 the cafe was significantly extended to include a restaurant and a large reception area. The cafe seats about 150, most diners choosing to dine Champs Elysee-style and watch the world go by.

SCAMPI ALLA GRIGLIE

You'll need 16 fresh scampi cut into halves.

Combine:
½ cup olive oil
4 cloves garlic, crushed
1 tablespoon parsley
juice of 1 lemon
salt and ground black pepper to taste

Baste scampi with this mixture and rotate on a hot grill for approximately 3 minutes.

Serve on a bed of lettuce and garnish with chopped parsley and lemon wedges.

Serves 4.

SCALOPPINI CON CARCIOFI

In a pan with 1 tablespoon heated butter, fry 750 g (1½ lb) thinly sliced and floured veal scallops. When golden brown on both sides add 1 glass dry white wine and reduce the heat.

Add:
8 halved artichoke hearts (canned variety will do)
1 cup cream
2 tablespoons chopped parsley
pinch of grated parmesan cheese
ground black pepper and salt to taste

Serve with potatoes baked in their jackets and lemon wedges.

Serves 4.

FETTUCCINE CON BROCCOLI

In boiling *salted water* cook *750 g (1½ lb) home-made pasta* until 'al dente' (until it floats). This takes about 3 minutes.

Strain and rinse in cold water.

In a pan heat *olive oil* to coat the base, and add:
2 cups steamed broccoli flowerettes
the fettuccine
½ cup fresh cream
⅓ cup grated parmesan cheese
1 tablespoon chopped parsley
salt and fresh ground *black pepper* to taste.

Combine gently and serve immediately.

Serves 4.

THE BREAD AND CHEESE SHOP

Open for breakfast, lunch and take-away seven days a week, Bannister Street's Bread and Cheese Shop started business in 1984. Partners Jeanette Lightboun and Anne Woollett make much of the delicious food on the premises and are assisted by the close proximity of a bread wholesaler.

NORFOLK PATTIES

So named because Anne lives in nearby Norfolk Street.
In a large bowl combine:
4 cups wholemeal breadcrumbs
1 cup sunflower seeds
½ cup poppy seeds
1 cup pumpkin seeds
1 cup pine nuts
1 cup grated carrot
1 cup chopped capsicum
1 cup chopped onion
5 eggs
salt and *pepper* to taste
1 teaspoon herbs of choice
Mix with the hands and shape into patties.
Deep fry in good quality *oil* for 5 minutes.
Drain and serve with home-made chutney.

To The Ladies of the Colony
O. K. Congdon has much pleasure in intimating to the Ladies of Western Australia The arrival of his Summer Shipment of Seasonable Goods per *Strathmore*, now being landed and opened daily.

The assortment comprises every article of attire requisite for Ladies Summer Wear.

Fremantle newspaper advertisement, 22 January 1869

PRINCESS COFFEE LOUNGE

Judith and Gerry Terrahan acquired the Princess Coffee Lounge in Market Street in 1980, and serve delighted customers with delicious dishes made on the premises.
The following are two of their favourites.

CHEESE AND HAM MUFFINS

Put in a bowl:
1 cup plain flour
2 teaspoons baking powder
pinch cayenne pepper
1 cup grated cheese
2 slices ham, finely chopped

Add 1 beaten egg, combined with enough milk to fill a cup, and mix well.
Put in greased muffin tins and bake at 200°C (400°F) for 15 minutes.
Cool on a wire rack.

FIVE SPICE APRICOT DRUMSTICKS

In a bowl combine these ingredients for the marinade:
2 tablespoons honey
½ cup soy sauce
2 tablespoons brown sugar
½ cup tomato sauce
2 cups chicken stock
2 teaspoons 5-spice powder
2.5 cm (1 in) grated fresh ginger
1 × 425 ml can apricot nectar

Marinate 8 drumsticks or 12–14 chicken wings for several hours.
Bake in a moderate oven 180°C (350°F) in an open baking dish in the marinade for about 1 hour, turning often.
Serves 4.

GOLDEN PINK PUNCH

An easy, delicious, health-giving drink from The Health Hut, which also contributed the following wholesome recipes.
Blend:
2 cups milk
6 strawberries
1 *peach*, peeled and chopped
Serves 1.

LENTIL AND VEGETABLE SOUP

In a large saucepan combine:
2 cups brown lentils
½ cup chopped onion
¼ cup diced celery
½ cup diced carrots
½ cup diced potatoes
1 *garlic clove*, minced
1 teaspoon salt
1 tablespoon olive oil
1 small *tomato*, chopped
8 cups cold water
Bring to the boil and simmer 35 to 50 minutes.
Serves 6.

FROZEN BANANA ICE-CREAM

First freeze 3 medium *bananas*, peeled.
Blend the bananas with:
½ cup skimmed milk
1 teaspoon vanilla essence
2 tablespoons *coconut* (optional)
When smooth, serve at once.

As an alternative, try:
½ cup strawberries ⎫
½ cup chopped pineapple ⎬ frozen
1 banana ⎭
Blend as before with milk and vanilla essence.
Note: 1½ cups of any frozen fruit may be used.

CULLEY'S

Culley's for Afternoon Tea
Alexandra Cakes and Pastry
Cooked Meats
Iced and Cool Drinks
Opposite Station
Cottesloe Beach. Phone 629

The Fremantle Times
10 October 1919

Soon after the establishment of Culley's at Cottesloe, the business moved to 116 High Street, Fremantle, and has been there ever since. Darrell Culley is the third generation of the family to work in the tea rooms — which has the distinction of being the first in the area.

VANILLA SLICES

Specialising in home-made goodies, Culley's serves many perennial favourites including vanilla slices. Chef Steve Burwood advised that his kitchen staff normally makes five dozen at a time. This recipe (for half that quantity) can be made on a tray about 45 cm x 35 cm (18 in x 14 in), or two smaller trays.

Prepare the *custard*:
Combine in a saucepan:
250 g (8 oz) sugar
125 g (4 oz) butter
9 cups water
Heat to boiling point then whisk through until the custard thickens:
250 g (8 oz) milk powder ⎫
405 g (13 oz) cornflour ⎪
1 egg ⎬ combined
vanilla essence (few drops) ⎪
yellow colouring ⎭

While still hot, pour onto *cooked puff pastry halves*, sit remaining halves on top and set aside to cool. It's a good idea to put a weight on top to firm the slices — make sure it's not too heavy to squash them!

When cold ice with *water icing* — white or pink — spreading on while the icing is still runny.

Cut into slices.

OYSTER BEDS RESTAURANT

So popular is this seafood restaurant on the water that a summertime headcount shows an average of 2000 diners a week and 1300 to 1500 a week in winter.

Dawn Davies, the owner since 1966, has established an enviable reputation since her impulse purchase of what was then an old tin shack with oyster racks underneath.

Dawn has had some very interesting experiences with customers and staff since opening the restaurant. Her favourite story concerns one of her early chefs who, believing Dawn to be the intended victim of evil spirits, appeared half naked about 10 pm and commenced to conduct a ceremony to keep the spirits away.

After a grizzly performance during which he threaded himself with skewers, had a kitchen maid shove them into his back, and pushed forks every which way, he removed himself to reappear soon afterwards — beautifully dressed and expressing hopes that the spirits had gone!

Following are some favourites from the restaurant.

COBBLER AND GREEN PEPPERCORNS

Cobbler is a famous fish in the West, but other kinds could be substituted in this recipe.

Combine in a pan:
2 teaspoons butter, melted
2 teaspoons lemon juice
2 teaspoons Pernod
5 coriander leaves
10 g (¼ oz) green peppercorns

Bring to the boil and drop in *half a large pear*, thinly sliced.

Cook lightly, remove from pan and set aside.

In another pan with a little *butter*, brown:
185 g (6 oz) cobbler
60 g (2 oz) fresh prawn flesh

Finish cooking in the pan juices and serve immediately, with pear slices arranged around the seafood.

Serves 1.

CRAB AND PEAR ENTREE

While the Oyster Beds restaurant uses fresh cooked *blue swimmer crabs* for this delicacy, good quality canned crabmeat may be substituted.

If fresh crabs are available, cook about ten minutes in a pot with:
fish stock to cover
sprinkle of *fresh or dried herbs*
salt to taste

Allow to cool.

Arrange crabmeat on individual plates with very finely sliced ripe *pears* (skin on).

Serve this *sauce* on the side:
Combine:
½ cup tomato puree
½ cup thin cream
2 teaspoons Worcestershire sauce
2 teaspoons vodka

Serves 4.

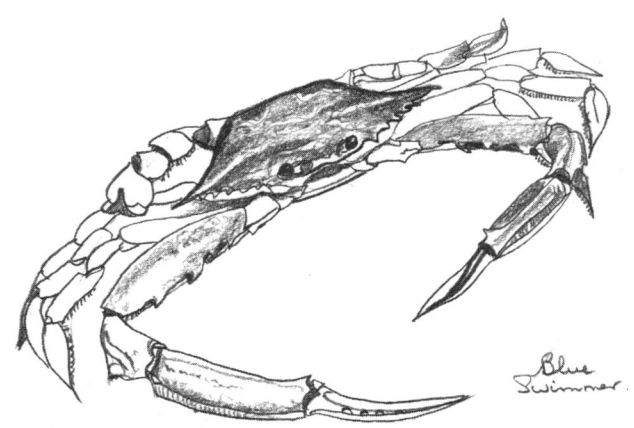

CEVICHE

Mexican Kitchen, one of Fremantle's best known restaurants, supplied this popular marinated raw fish recipe and the following famous dip recipe as well.

Cut *1 kg (2 lb)* fresh ocean *fish fillets* into cubes and marinate for about one hour in a bowl with *1 cup lime or lemon juice*.

Before serving, mix in:
1 cup finely chopped onion
2 firm tomatoes, finely chopped
½ cup vinegar
¼ cup salad oil
½ teaspoon oregano
salt and *pepper* to taste

Serve in chilled *lettuce leaves*.
Serves 6.

GUACAMOLE

Great with pre-dinner drinks.

In a bowl, mash the flesh of *2 very ripe avocados* with a fork and blend in:
½ small onion, finely chopped
1 firm ripe tomato, finely chopped
3 tablespoons lemon or lime juice
½ clove garlic, finely chopped (or to taste)
salt to taste

Cover and chill.

Serve with *corn chips*.

* P·O·P·U·L·A·R P·U·B·S *

Fremantle has pubs galore — many of them built in a grand manner to cater for the gold rush trade of the late nineteenth century. Some of them are presented in this section, with accompanying mouth-watering recipes.

FEDERAL HOTEL

One of the numerous hotels in Fremantle listed by the National Trust, the Federal was built in 1887 by James Herbert Junior on the site once occupied by a cottage and bakery owned by the Herbert family.

In years gone by, the hotel's popularity was enhanced by its distance from 'the clanging of the gaol and the bustle of High Street' and the fact that it sported 'one of the finest billiard tables' in Western Australia.

From its first days until the 1960s, the hotel was a popular holiday destination for country people and overseas visitors. Its most hectic days occurred during the gold rush when optimistic gold-diggers flocked to the area.

The hotel has many stories of characters in residence, and rumour has it that a bar upstairs was once used for 'ladies of ill-repute' to privately entertain male passengers and officers from visiting ships.

Mick Vodanovich took over the management of the hotel in 1981 and had it extensively redecorated. Affectionately dubbed 'Mick the Fiddler' he made the Federal a popular music venue, providing live entertainment each week night.

Early in 1986 management of the hotel changed hands.

Today, hosts Tim and Kay Cross ensure that the Federal remains popular with patrons, and the day I dined there the Raffles-style restaurant with potted palms aplenty under the lovely glass-roofed courtyard was crowded with appreciative customers. The food was superb and the following recipes were provided by the hotel chef.

CREAM OF GARLIC PRAWNS

Cook turning together in hot *oil* just covering the base of a frying pan:
10 large green prawns, peeled and deveined
3 tablespoons finely chopped garlic

Cook only until prawns turn pink — they will be tough if overcooked.

Add:
3 tablespoons white sauce
2 tablespoons cream

Serve on a bed of *rice*.

Serves 2 as an entree.

PECAN PIE

Base:
Into a bowl sift *2 cups plain flour* and *1 tablespoon icing sugar*. Rub in *185 g (6 oz) butter* and mix to a firm dough with *1 teaspoon lemon juice* and *1-2 teaspoons water* — or enough to bind the ingredients. Knead lightly until smooth and refrigerate for 30 minutes. Roll dough to fit the base of one greased 23 cm (9 in) flan tin or swiss roll tin. Place pastry around the side of the tin without stretching. Refrigerate a further 15 minutes. Place greaseproof paper over the base of the pastry, sprinkle with raw *rice* and bake in a moderately hot oven 190°C (375°F) for 15 minutes. Remove paper and rice. Sprinkle *185g (6 oz) pecan nuts* evenly over the pastry base.

Filling:
In a saucepan melt *90 g (3 oz) butter* and stir in:
½ cup golden syrup or treacle
⅓ cup brown sugar, firmly packed
2 eggs, beaten with a fork
¼ cup plain flour ⎤ sifted together
¼ cup self-raising flour ⎦
Stir until smooth and pour over the pecan nuts. Place the flan tin on a flat tray and bake in a moderate oven, 180°C (350°F) for 30 minutes or until firm. Serve warm or cold with *whipped cream* or *ice-cream*.

Boat Building
The undersigned begs to inform the Public that he has resumed the above business, in all its branches, and hopes to obtain the same degree of patronage with which he was formerly favoured. Large and small Boats built and repaired at the shortest notice and on the most reasonable terms.

T. Mews, Senior
The Inquirer, 21 January 1852.

THE ESPLANADE HOTEL

Having recently had $16 million spent on a facelift and extensions, the Esplanade today looks quite different from the original hotel that was designed by architect C. L. Oldham and erected in 1897.

The developers aimed to retain the character of the old 'Nade' (pronounced Nard) as it was commonly known. Situated on a prize site in Fremantle — on the park, and close to the water and the yachting and sailing fraternity — the hotel has long been a people place, 'the fishermen's hotel'. 'See you at the Nade' has long been a catch phrase of fishermen from Darwin to Albany.

Reopened in grand new style in 1986, the Esplanade is now transformed into a four-star 142-room hotel with a swimming pool in a central courtyard covered by a clear dome, a restaurant and a garden tavern. Still reflecting the turn-of-the-century architecture of the original hotel, the two-storey building features timber verandahs on all street frontages.

With walls of limestone and brick and a corrugated iron roof, the Esplanade was typical of many hotels erected during the gold-rush period to accommodate the sudden population increase. A distinctive feature of the original building was the ornate corner tower which has been retained.

Close to the beach and Fremantle Swimming Baths, the Esplanade was always a popular family hotel. It makes the most of 'The Fremantle Doctor' — the cooling seaside breeze that blows regularly during the summer months. (During my own summertime stopovers 'The Fremantle Doctor', while certainly cooling the frazzled brow, sometimes seemed more like a roaring gale! Old-time brochures circulated by the Fremantle City Council emphasised 'the veritable pleasure ground of life-giving and healing essences derived from the ozone-laden atmosphere'.)

With the America's Cup heralding a new era in the city's tourism, the Esplanade Hotel, providing the only luxury accommodation, will no doubt be a focal point in Fremantle for a long time to come.

SCALLOPS FEUILLETE

Using *4 puff pastry sheets* measuring about 5 cm x 10 cm (2 in x 4 in) and 5 mm (¼ in) thick, brush with *milk* and bake in a hot oven for 15–20 minutes. Keep warm. Cut each piece in half.

In a saucepan put:
32 fresh scallops
6 cups white wine

Poach gently for 1 minute and add:
1 carrot, cut into julienne strips
2 sticks celery, cut into julienne strips
1 leek, cut into julienne strips
1 tablespoon chopped fresh tarragon

Cook only a few seconds — vegetables should retain crispness.

Remove the scallops and vegetables from the liquid, arrange on puff pastry shells and keep warm. Reserve 3 cups of liquid and reduce by boiling rapidly until slightly thickened. Stir in *215 g (7 oz) butter* and whisk vigorously. Pour over the scallops and vegetables, place other half of puff pastry on top and garnish with fresh tarragon.

Serves 4.

HOTEL FREMANTLE

The Hotel Fremantle was built around a cottage of 1830's vintage. It is only in recent years that documents were discovered suggesting the hotel could have been the original home owned by Mr W. O. Moore, one of the first merchants in Fremantle and a member of the Legislative Council in Western Australia's early years.

The boom years following discovery of gold in the state saw the present three-storey section of the hotel built out onto the street in 1898 with only one wing of the old structure remaining. The roof line was altered sometime last century but the window shape and placement indicate a Georgian style adapted for the first colonial buildings.

When it reopened for business, the hotel was the largest and best appointed in Fremantle. In December 1898, the *Morning Herald* reported:

There are 100 rooms, furnished and arranged on the most modern principles and with perfect sanitary arrangements by which all refuse and waste water is carried direct to the sea.

There is a first class billiard saloon with two Alocks tables. This hotel supplies a long-felt want in the Port and the position could not be improved on for the convenience of travellers arriving and departing by either rail or sea!

In 1985 the hotel, with the little cottage still an integral part of it, had extensive renovations carried out. Its owners, brothers Stan and Brett Lenton, initiated a massive redevelopment project to restore the Fremantle to its original Victorian elegance.

Bedrooms were remodelled, and the dining room became one of Fremantle's most popular.

In 1986 the hotel was leased to Lion Brewery (N.Z.) and further renovations were carried out. The kitchen has been modernised and the dining area increased to include a paved courtyard restaurant. The former 'Arches' restaurant has been renamed 'Cobb & Co' to commemorate the important part played by the famous coach company in the early days of Australian settlement.

The following recipe is a New Zealand favourite from the Fremantle Hotel.

CANTERBURY CROCKPOT SILVERSIDE

Ingredients include New Zealand's award-winning Steinlager beer. In fact a poster holding pride of place in the hotel bottle shop reads: 'Steinlager (N.Z.) confirmed the best lager in the world. Overall winner of the Brewing Industry International Awards — Burton-on-Trent, England.'

In a crockpot put 2 kg (4 lb) corned silverside

Add:
6 small onions
6 small carrots
2 bayleaves
1 cup water
1 340 ml bottle beer (Steinlager)

Cook on high for 5–6 hours, depending on the size of the meat. It's very tasty!

Serves 6–8.

THE NATIONAL HOTEL

Like many of Fremantle's old pubs, the National was built in the late 1880s and seems as busy now as it was in days of the gold-rush boom.

The National's builder was a Mr Collins, whose descendants continue to live in the area. Its first proprietor was W. Conroy who advertised in 1887 'Good Accommodation — Wines, Beers, and Spirits of the Best Quality kept in Stock'.

An early advertisement appearing in the *Fremantle Districts Sentinel* claimed 'First Class Table and Accommodation at Moderate Prices — Special rates for families' and invited 'Goldfields and Country visitors when in town call in'.

In the early twentieth century the pub was a favourite drinking spot for men who worked on the wharves. As one old-timer recently recalled: 'In those days we used to work hard on the wharves and drink hard in the pub. Because of the hard work nobody got drunk — and fights were scarce because the pub was kept in pretty good nick.

'Nowadays', he went on, 'the waterside job is so easy it only takes a few beers and the young chaps fall over.'

The National had a narrow escape from destruction when in 1975 a fire swept through the top floor.

In 1983 the old pub was given an external facelift, and internal renovation was carried out in 1986. With the assistance of advice from the National Trust and the Fremantle Council, its owners, John and Tinks Stabinowsky, have restored the upstairs dining area to take advantage of its beautiful traditional features.

Recently, after many years in the hotel business, John and Tinks have gone into semi-retirement. Their son, Robert, is now the National's licensee and his wife, Margaret, assists him with managing the hotel.

Irish barman Michael Egan has been working with the Stabinowsky family for fifteen years. He started with them at the Commercial Hotel and with successive moves to different pubs, Michael has moved with them! Every St Patrick's Day he dresses as a leprechaun and jumps around the bar selling green beer!

The following recipes were provided by the chef of the National's restaurant.

FILO CHICKEN

In a flameproof casserole marinate *6 skinned chicken breasts* in *soy sauce* for 30 minutes. Partly cook for a few minutes over medium heat then thicken the juices with *1 tablespoon cornflour* mixed with a little cold *water*. Allow to cool.

Wrap each chicken breast in a large folded sheet of *filo pastry* with a sprinkle of chopped *garlic* and *parsley*. Place, folded side under, onto a greased baking dish and brush each with cooking *oil*.

Bake in a moderate oven 180°C (350°F) until brown and cooked, 25–30 minutes.

Serves 6.

PRAWN CUTLETS

Using *6 large green prawns*, peel, devein and slit open. Sprinkle with a little *salt*, roll in *plain flour*, dip in *1 beaten egg* and press firmly (with the palm of the hand) into fine, dry *breadcrumbs*.

In a pan, heat cooking *oil* to cover the base of the pan and when moderately hot, cook cutlets one at a time, turning once.

Don't overcook — just until each side is a light golden brown.

Drain and serve.

Serves 1 as a main course.

Fremantle Memories
Laurel and Frank (Collins) deplore the loss of hundreds of jobs on the waterfront over the last two decades.

'We often wonder what went wrong — we made a lot of friends among the lumpers. We also befriended many people in the Customs, Port Authority, and the shipping firms.'

Asked about memories of Fremantle, the couple nominated brewery lorries with solid tyres rattling down the jarrah-block paving of the High Street, and the old Women's Home — now the W.A. Museum and Arts Centre.

Fremantle Gazette, 6 July 1983

THE SAIL AND ANCHOR

Originally known as the Freemason's Hotel, this delightful building has been classified by the National Trust.

First owned by James Herbert Senior, the two-storey hotel of rendered stone and brick was designed by F. W. Burwell whose works also included Dalkieth Opera House, the Fremantle Oval Pavilion and warehouses for Burns Philp and Co.

In the 1860s the Freemason's Hotel in Fremantle was inordinately proud to advertise that it had 'a bathroom'!

James Herbert advertised in the *Herald West Australian Almanac and Commercial Directory* for 1872 that he had 'the LARGEST and MOST CONVENIENT HOTEL in Fremantle, replete with every Comfort and Accommodation . . .

'Good Stabling and an Attentive Ostler'.

He was a proud manufacturer of lemonade, soda water, tonic and other aerated waters and an 1878 advertisement in the *West Australian* makes fascinating reading:

> J.A.H., in returning thanks for the patronage hitherto extended to him, begs to inform the public that he now uses in his hotel CHEAVIN'S CELEBRATED WATER FILTERS and CODD'S PATENT BOTTLES, and can confidently recommend his Aerated Drinks as equal to any that are imported.
>
> The advantages of pure water are inestimable in a sanitary point of view, the organic and mineral impurities (remaining even in boiled water) being the source of the most deadly diseases. In connection with aerated drinks, it not only adds a more pleasant flavour than unfiltered water to the drink, but acts as a refrigerator, which is a great acquisition.

From aerated waters to beer brewing is a big jump, but that's the brew for which this beautifully restored hotel is now justly famous.

Operated by Philip Seston, and renamed the Sail and Anchor, the restored hotel reopened its doors in 1985. Patrons are now able to enjoy ale made on the premises by the Anchor Brewing Company which is wedged between the ground floor bars thus enabling those interested to view the beer-making process!

The hotel's factory restoration, costing $300,000, took eight months to complete and won for it the prestigious Architecture Award (W.A.). The Sail and Anchor also won a commendation for the restoration's authenticity.

Upstairs, Mason's Brasserie, managed jointly by Robert May and Henry Bromberg, wins daily accolades from delighted diners — fine French food served in an authentic Victorian setting excites the most jaded palate.

The Sail and Anchor is a must on every tourist's itinerary.

QUENELLES OF SNAPPER WITH SWEET PEPPER SAUCE

Amounts can be adjusted to suit individual tastes.

Trim *500 g (1 lb) snapper* fillets of any bones and chop roughly.

Blend in a food processor and add:
2 *egg whites*
salt and *pepper* to taste

Blend again, and chill the mixture for 30 minutes.

Gradually add *1¼ cups cream*, beating with wooden spoon.

This mixture may be stored in the refrigerator for several days.

To cook, shape quenelles by pressing the mixture between two tablespoons and rolling one spoon after the other. Place in boiling *salted water*, boil 5 minutes and remove with a slotted spoon.

Arrange on sweet pepper sauce on plates and decorate each with sprigs of fennel.

Sweet pepper sauce:
In a pan melt *1 tablespoon butter* and cook until just soft:
2 *red capsicums*, seeded and finely chopped
4 *spring onions*, finely chopped

Add *2 tablespoons sweet paprika* and cook for 1 minute. Moisten with a small quantity of *white wine or dry vermouth*. Blend in a food processor.

Transfer to a pan, add *1¼ cups cream* and reduce until it thickens.

Season to taste.

Serves 4 as an entree.

LAMB FILLETS ON A BED OF LEEKS WITH BEAUJOLAIS SAUCE

Finely chop 2 *leeks* and cook in a pan with ½ *tablespoon heated butter* just until wilted. Add a little *water or white wine* to prevent burning, and cook until soft.

Add 2 *tablespoons cream* and cook until absorbed (about 2 minutes). Season to taste.

Dust 6 *lamb fillets* in *flour* and saute in ½ *tablespoon heated butter* in a pan until well browned. Add *1 cup beaujolais*, light red or rose, and stir to deglaze the pan. Remove the lamb when cooked and keep warm. Reduce the sauce by about half. Season and just before serving, swirl through a knob of *butter*.

To serve, put equal quantities of leeks in the centre of each plate, place 3 fillets on each plate and pour a small quantity of sauce around the leeks.

Serves 2.

THE AULD MUG TAVERN
(Cleopatra Hotel)

'Cleo's' as it was affectionately known, was named after a sailing ship of the 1880s, captained by a Sussex sailor called Fothergill. According to Ted Fothergill, a descendant living in Fremantle, the captain built the Cleopatra Hotel in High Street 'but died some years later from diseases related to drinking the hotel's profits'.

Built in 1895, the hotel advertised its shady garden drinking area in much the same way as air-conditioning is advertised today. Impressions from 1901 read thus:

> One of the oldest and best known hotels in Fremantle is the Cleopatra, which is centrally situated in High Street and which provides excellent accommodation for the many visitors who avail themselves of its hospitality.
>
> There is a shady verandah, well provided with easy chairs and lounges, all around the house ...
>
> The building itself, which has a pleasant lawn in front, is a two-story [sic] one with a quaint, old-fashioned air that tells of comfort and quiet and good nut-brown ale or cheering wine within.

That Cleopatra was demolished in 1906 and the present hotel erected the same year. Renovations in 1970 saw preservation of its original character, with new internal arches duplicating those on the exterior.

In 1985 further changes were made to the old pub. Under new ownership comprising two Australians, Arthur Bull and Rick Rodereda, and an American, Jack Farrell (dockside operations manager for *America II*, a U.S. America's Cup hope), the hotel was renovated for the purpose of attracting tourists to the America's Cup races in 1986–87.

Known as the Auld Mug Tavern, it has become a popular 'watering hole' for the yacht crews, providing a spacious and welcoming dining and bar area on the ground floor. Patrons are offered an extensive range of bar snacks and a small a la carte menu.

Chef Meric Wallace enjoys his work, and with a name which is a derivation of the spice turmeric, it's little wonder that he has been keen on cooking since boyhood.

The following recipes are his own creations.

CHICKEN ROXANNE

Chef Merrick Wallace named this dish for his daughter.

You'll need 2 *boned chicken breasts*, available as fillets in many poultry shops.

Bash fillets to flatten them, season, dust with *flour* and cook gently in a pan with a little heated *butter* until beginning to crisp, then turn and crisp other side.

When nearly done, add 2 *wine glasses moselle*. Boil rapidly to reduce liquid — this ensures the chicken is thoroughly cooked.

Add about 12 *large green prawns* and 1 *clove garlic*, finely chopped.

Stir in ¾ *cup cream*, reduce and there's the sauce.

Serve with *rice pilaf* and a *green salad* or fresh *broccoli*.

Serves 2.

THE AULD MUG'S WEST COAST SALAD

A modified version of a Swedish dish, this should be prepared just prior to eating.

Combine in a salad bowl:
1 *lettuce*, shredded
1 *cup fresh garden peas*
1 *cup canned champignons*
1 *cup whole school prawns*, cooked and shelled
salt and *pepper* to taste

Toss with *seafood dressing*:
Combine:
⅓ *cup tomato sauce*
1 *tablespoon tomato paste*
1 *tablespoon brandy*
⅓ *cup cream*

Serve with *lemon wedges*.

Serves 4.

NORFOLK HOTEL

A small, quality hotel, which substantially enhances the attractions of Fremantle, the Norfolk opened for business in 1985, and looks set to become something of an institution for both locals and visitors.

The original hotel on the site was the Oddfellows, built by J. A. Davies in 1887, a few years before the gold rush boom — and while it had had several refurbishings over the years, it was in a very sad state of repair when the current owners, Wayne and Robyn Donaldson, decided to buy it.

Nevertheless, they had eyed it enviously for a number of years before the opportunity came to them to purchase it and thus fulfil their dream to create 'a lovely, gentle, Fremantle-style hostelry'.

The building alterations they have already undertaken include the construction of an attractive paved courtyard — necessitating the demolition of about one third of the old hotel. Deciduous trees

have been planted in the courtyard and now provide shade in summer and allow the sun to shine through in winter. To establish the trees, Mr Donaldson walled up about one third of the basement and filled it with dirt and manure to ensure a long healthy life for the trees atop!

The courtyard, well sheltered from the elements, provides a pavement atmosphere for people to dine and drink while still within licensed premises.

The interior bar and dining area is fresh, warm and inviting — the bar is made of beautiful Oregon timber originally used as ballast on whaling ships from the U.S.A. The timber had been stored all those years since in a Fremantle warehouse.

Accommodation is limited to eleven rooms with guests enjoying a friendly family atmosphere.

Recognised as one of Fremantle's most attractive hotels, the Norfolk has every chance of achieving its owners' aim 'to provide Fremantle with the best little pub in Australia'.

FRESH CRAB

Beautiful blue swimmer crabs are caught in Cockburn Sound, a few kilometres offshore.

The Norfolk Hotel is supplied by an elderly fisherman who goes out regularly for crays and crabs, some of which weigh 500 g (1 lb) each. Smaller crabs are used for seafood platters.

To prepare, drop *crab* or crabs into heavily salted boiling *water*, bring back to boil and cook 7 minutes.

Lift out and put under cold water to stop the cooking process.

Serve with *brown vinegar, black pepper, seafood sauce, rolls* and *French salad*.

* A·R·T·S & C·R·A·F·T·S *

With such an attractive old-worlde atmosphere it was inevitable that Fremantle would become a mecca for creative people. Some of their culinary creations are included in this section.

FREMANTLE MUSEUM AND ARTS CENTRE

Plans were afoot in the early 1960s to demolish the building that now houses the Fremantle Museum and Arts Centre. Admittedly, at that time it was in a sad state of disrepair but thanks to a dedicated group led by the late Sir Frederick Samson, a program of restoration and renovation commenced and the building's future was assured.

It was built by convicts in the early 1860s as a Lunatic Asylum, mainly to house those prisoners who suffered mental illness, many as a result of transportation effects, alienation from family and distances from home. The first patients were admitted in 1865.

Overcrowding led to the addition of the south wing (now the Arts Centre) in 1897.

In 1866 the Superintendent reported:

> Both male and female lunatics have large dining rooms, separate from the sleeping apartments, these latter wards are also spacious and lofty and well ventilated. There is a large exercising yard at the back of the building, with a covered shed to protect from the sun. In this yard also there is a large wash-house in which the female lunatics do a great deal of the prison washing (500 pieces per week average); and also an arranged kitchen, in which the whole cooking for the Asylum is done.

The same year the Asylum was transferred from imperial to colonial control and responsibility for it was given to the Superintendent of Public Works, George Temple-Poole.

With accommodation again crowded, a new wing was added in 1890, and George Temple-Poole designed a further addition which was completed in 1894.

Overcrowding continued to be a problem, and in 1900 the Asylum was condemned when two cases of typhoid were reported from within its vicinity. However, it was not until 1909 that all the inmates had been moved to new premises at Claremont and the Asylum, at that time the second largest building in Fremantle, was left to rot.

In 1916 it was decided to use the newer wings as a home for elderly women and soon the whole building was back in use. It served as the Old Women's Home until 1942.

From 1942 until the end of the war it became the headquarters for the U.S. Navy base in Fremantle. With very little maintenance it soon fell again into a sad state and at the end of the war its demolition seemed inevitable.

During the 1950s the Fremantle Technical College held classes in the south wing, thus giving the old building another reprieve. In 1957 the Mayor of Fremantle, Sir Frederick Samson, put a proposal to the State Government and City of Fremantle that the building should be converted into a Mariners' Museum and Arts Centre. The Government refused to finance the project, and the building continued to deteriorate.

Then in 1963 came an inspection by the Chairman of the National Trust of Great Britain, the Earl of Euston, who told Sir Frederick: 'Don't you let them demolish this building — it is the best example of Colonial Gothic architecture in Australia today'.

Finally in 1965 Government assistance was assured and the conversion began. The Museum was opened to the public in 1970. The Arts Centre was opened in 1972.

The Fremantle Museum houses priceless maritime relics from the *Batavia*, wrecked off the western coast in 1629, and holds many other displays pertaining to early settlement.

Other parts of the building house exhibitions of art, jewellery, pottery and painting, and there is even a delightful courtyard coffee shop where visitors may sit and ponder the stories of the ghosts that are said to haunt the building!

PUMPKIN FRUIT CAKE

This is a sample of the delicious array of home-made coffee-time specials served at the Arts Centre Coffee Shop.

In a saucepan combine:
500 g (1 lb) mixed fruit
1 cup brown sugar
1 tablespoon orange juice
125 g (4 oz) butter

Bring to the boil, stirring, and boil for 8 minutes.

Allow to cool for 1 hour then add, in order:
1 cup warm mashed cooked pumpkin
2 eggs, lightly beaten
2 cups self-raising flour

Turn into a greased cake tin and bake in a moderate oven for about 45 minutes or until cooked when tested.

POTTERS WORKSHOP AND GALLERY

This enterprise, made famous by internationally renowned potter Joan Campbell, is located in an old seaside building which was the original bond store for the early settlement. It later became the Harbour and Light Department's boatbuilding workshop.

Thought to be the second oldest building in Fremantle, this simple limestone structure is situated close to the Round House.

Joan Campbell has always had an affection for the building and, when she outgrew her Perth location in 1975, she eagerly relocated her business in it. The atmosphere provides a wonderful working environment for artists who 'need to be amongst life'.

Joan keeps the workshop open to the public and it has become highly regarded as a training place for young potters. For ten years Joan has been training people from all over the world. Her courses usually last one year.

In the self-supporting workshop, the five or six trainees take turns in cooking lunches. Joan believes that 'eating together is very important to happiness'.

There is no competition between the trainees and, invariably, the conclusion of each course brings expressions of sadness that it's all over.

To increase its involvement with the local community, the workshop holds two 'community days' each year — these are very popular. For the city's fiftieth birthday all the locals were invited for breakfast. Over 60 kilograms of rolled oats from the mill were cooked and porridge was being served well into the afternoon.

Another time during 'open house' the workshop ran out of soup and some kindly locals, who could see what was happening, raced home and returned laden with buckets of soup.

For Joan Campbell, Fremantle is all about friendliness. While she finds enjoyment and stimulation in the Fremantle scene, locals and visitors find her contributions not only artistic, but educational, hospitable and ever-interesting.

Her work is displayed in galleries throughout Australia and New Zealand and in London's Victoria and Albert Museum.

The following recipes are favourites prepared and served at her workshop.

PASTA WITH MARINARA SAUCE

This is a favourite lunch at the Potters Workshop. With the fish markets alongside there is a ready availability of fresh seafood and fettuccine is made daily in Fremantle.

In a large frying pan with *2 tablespoons hot oil*, fry gently for a few seconds:

2 tablespoons chopped fresh parsley or basil

1 or 2 cloves garlic, finely chopped

Stir in *3 small calamari*, cleaned and sliced.

Add *1 cup white wine* and simmer about 10 minutes.

Add *1 x 440 g (14 oz) can whole peeled tomatoes*, chopped, plus the juice from the can and when bubbling add *250 g (8 oz) green king prawns*, shelled and deveined.

Cook about 5 minutes, add *250 g (8 oz) sliced fresh scallops* and simmer for just a few minutes longer. Season to taste.

Serve over *250 g (8 oz) green fettuccine* freshly cooked and accompanied by crusty *Italian bread* and *cheese*.

Serves 6–8.

SALMON MOUSSE

A delicious dish served as part of a Potters Workshop lunch. Combine ¾ *tablespoon gelatine* with 2 *tablespoons cold water* and set aside.

In the top of a double saucepan combine:
1 *tablespoon flour*
1½ *tablespoons sugar*

Add:
1 *teaspoon salt*
1 *teaspoon mustard*
sprinkle of cayenne pepper
2 *eggs*

Mix well and add:
¾ *cup warm milk*
½ *cup white vinegar*
1½ *tablespoons butter*

Cook in the double saucepan over boiling water, stirring constantly until thick. Cool slightly, stir in gelatine mixture then add:
1 *large (or 2 small) cans red salmon*, drained
½ *cup thickened cream*, unwhipped

Pour into an oiled mould and set in the refrigerator.

Serve with *cucumber sauce* or just a light *green salad* if following with pasta marinara.

Serves 6–8.

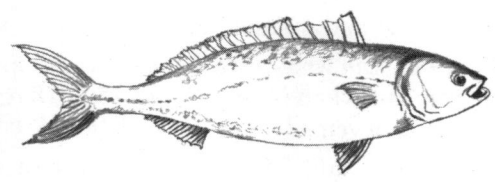

FREMANTLE MARKETS

In 1897, a competition was held to choose a suitable design for the markets. It was won by architects Oldham and Eales, and the foundation stone was laid the same year by the Premier, Sir John Forrest.

The building became a fine commercial complex. At first, a wholesale food market operated in the building, open Friday and Saturday. It later became a packing and distributing centre for a firm named Scanlan and Simper — a window bearing the name remains in one wall as a reminder of the past.

Long-term residents recall that in the 1920s the markets were supplied with produce from market gardens in North Fremantle. Memories include the buying antics of Wing Kee, who had a vegetable round in the district, and Ah Sam, who owned a vegetable shop in Perth.

After a lengthy period of disuse, the markets were given a new lease of life when Wayne Donaldson leased the old building from the Fremantle City Council in 1975. The site was in a totally derelict state; however, he had eyed it for some years as a revitalised market in which authentic retail stalls could operate.It became the first venture of its kind in Western Australia.

Today, the massive old iron gates are still in place in the three main entrances. The bullnosed verandahs, removed in the 1950s because they were considered a traffic hazard, have been reconstructed and a Victorian atmosphere has been recreated.

It's wonderful! An exciting place, open Friday, Saturday and Sunday each week, it offers something for everyone.

Affectionately dubbed 'Freo Markets' it appeals not only for the character of the building itself, but for the top-quality merchandise offered within: arts, crafts, antiques, bric-a-brac, clothing, foods and spices. There is even an 1897 Coffee House. It's all there, under one rambling roof.

Some vendors have become so well known they now market goods state-wide. One such is Gervanet France — selling a delicious chicken liver pate made famous by Gerny Rousset and Marie-France Van Hall.

Also widely recognised for their excellence in quality and presentation are Harper and Whittingtons (Herb and Spice Merchants) and the authentic Coffee House run by the Morgan family.

Their recipes follow.

1897 COFFEE HOUSE

Established in 1897, this quaint and warmly welcoming coffee house at Fremantle Markets is run by Margaret Morgan and her daughter Christine. Authentic in every detail — even the ancient cash register — it was used as a setting for the highly successful Australian television series *A Fortunate Life* based on the autobiography of Western Australia's Albert Facey.

The following recipes are favourites served at the Coffee House.

CREAM OF WALNUT SOUP

In a saucepan put:
1 litre (4 cups) strong chicken stock or 8 chicken stock cubes in water
4 medium potatoes, peeled and sliced
Simmer until tender, cool and place in a blender.
Add *2 teaspoons chopped walnuts* and blend.
Just before serving add:
1¼ cups cream
2 tablespoons lemon juice
2 tablespoons finely chopped chives
salt and *pepper* to taste
Serve hot or cold.
Serves 6–8.

SPINACH SALAD WITH BACON DRESSING

In a bowl put:
1 bunch English spinach, washed and chopped
250 g (8 oz) mushrooms, sliced
6 spring onions, chopped
½ cup chopped walnuts or pecan nuts

Make this *dressing*:
Combine:
4 rashers bacon, derinded, chopped and fried until crisp and crunchy
½ cup yoghurt

Add to vinaigrette made with:
4 tablespoons olive oil
1 tablespoon vinegar
lemon juice to taste

Add as much as required to toss with salad.
Serves 6.

APPLE NUT PECAN CAKE

In a bowl beat *1 egg* into *125 g (4 oz) cooled melted butter*. Add *2 cooking apples*, peeled, cored and finely chopped.

Lightly fold in:
1½ cups self-raising flour
1 teaspoon bicarbonate of soda
1 teaspoon cinnamon   } sifted together
1 teaspoon allspice
½ teaspoon salt
1 cup roughly chopped pecan nuts

Spoon into a greased 20 cm (8 in) square tin and bake in a moderate oven 180°C (350°F) 45–55 minutes.

The cake is especially delicious served with *cream*.

HARPER AND WHITTINGTONS SPICE SHOP

Run by Donald and Peggy Whittington since 1975, this old-world herb and spice shop is a great attraction at the Fremantle Markets.

Peggy has always been interested in food preparation, and started Ceres vegetarian cafe in 1976. She loves the busy market atmosphere and finds the job 'gutsy and purposeful'. The following recipe makes good use of herbs and spices stocked at Harper and Whittingtons.

SQUID CURRY

In a large saucepan heat 3 *tablespoons ghee* (clarified butter) and in it saute 2 *large onions*, quartered and sliced, until golden.

Stir in:
4 *cloves garlic*, sliced
10 *curry leaves*, crushed
4 *teaspoons freshly ground cumin*
2 *teaspoons freshly ground turmeric*
1 *teaspoon ground chili* (optional)

Add:
½ *cup coconut cream*
3 *tablespoons freshly squeezed lemon juice*
500 g (1 lb) *squid (calamari) rings*
1 *large red capsicum*, sliced into strips
1 *large green capsicum*, sliced into strips

Simmer 20 minutes, stirring occasionally.

Store in refrigerator 24 hours.

Reheat and serve with *Basmati rice* and *pappadums*.

Serves 6–8.

Market Prices
Business continues brisk in the Fremantle Market at the early morning sales. Yesterday morning the vegetables were good and of a varied assortment. Prices were as follow: mint, parsley and radishes, sixpence per dozen bunches; tomatoes, threepence per pound; potatoes and onions, ten shillings per hundredweight; beans two pence per gallon; peas sixpence per gallon; eggs one shilling and sixpence per dozen.

Morning Herald, December 1898

BANNISTER STREET CRAFTWORKS

One of the most comprehensive craftsmen's workshops I've seen, the Bannister Street Craftworks operates as a co-operative. Established in 1979, it provides unique surroundings in which some of Western Australia's leading craftspeople produce, sell and take orders for their work.

The co-operative is situated in one of Fremantle's oldest warehouses which was saved from demolition when John Gordon, a local craftsman, initiated the idea for its use as a craft workshop. He was to become the co-operative's first foundation member.

The workshops include a blacksmith, glass engraver, potter, screen printing, handknits and woodwork.

Thousands of dollars have been spent to make the turn-of-the-century warehouse functional and improvements continue to be made.

An attractive tea garden at the rear of the workshops entices shoppers and browsers to spend more time enjoying this fascinating enterprise.

BEEF AND ORANGE SATE

Trim *1 kg (2 lb) thick skirt steak* and cut into cubes.
Place in a suitable container and mix with:
2 large cloves garlic, crushed
4 heaped teaspoons Malay curry powder
2 heaped teaspoons ground ginger
2 heaped teaspoons sugar
1 level teaspoon salt
1 sprig rosemary, broken up, or about 1 teaspoon dried rosemary
Pour over *orange juice concentrate* to just cover the lot.

Mark the container with the date and store in the refrigerator for up to 14 days and not less than six. Stir every day or so.

At cooking time, drain and lightly squeeze off any surplus marinade. Place meat in a chip basket (if you have one). Deep fry in very hot oil for 45–50 seconds — in order that the meat be properly sealed and not lose any juices, the oil must be smoking hot. The timing is crucial — after 50 seconds the meat will burn so it's advisable to use a stopwatch!

Serve on a bed of *rice*.

Serves 4.

TIMOTHY'S TOYS

Mary and Gordon Kay began operation in this charmingly reconstructed 1840s Croke Lane warehouse in 1983. Croke Lane, named for Captain Croke, a harbour master in the 1870s, was once called Dalgety Street, but following much confusion with a second Dalgety Street in East Fremantle, it was renamed.

The area was derelict when the Kays, looking for storage space, answered an advertisement for 'space to let'. Timothy's Toys — named for their young son — operates with the aim of creating unique and durable toys: 'special things for special people'.

Almost all of the toys are made on the premises, lovingly worked by Gordon with Mary's assistance in sanding and painting. Local crafts and imports make up the rest.

Admirably displayed in the lovely old warehouse are toys to delight both young and old. Being situated so close to the sea the place lends itself to maritime pieces — exquisitely carved miniature sailing craft and miniature canons vie for attention with racing cars, wooden horses, planes and trains. Most special of all the 'special things' are Gordon's exquisite little Scandinavian fishing boats, bought by customers from all over the world.

Timothy's Toys attracts groups of school children from all over Western Australia wishing to further their education in local crafts.

The Kays love Fremantle's old world atmosphere and plan to continue working there.

Mary loves cooking and the following recipes are some of her favourites.

CREAM OF CAULIFLOWER SOUP

Using a *medium sized cauliflower*, remove outside leaves, separate into branches, wash and cook until soft in very lightly *salted water*. Drain, puree and pass through a fine sieve.

Add this puree to *1¾ cups bouillon* and bring to the boil very gradually over low heat. Let simmer 15 minutes. Remove from the heat and add *a large glass of milk*. Taste for seasoning, and if too salty, add more milk. Add *125 g (4 oz) butter*, stirring as it melts.

To finish, add *4 egg yolks* beaten with *½ glass of water*, stirring over low heat until the soup thickens. Don't let it boil.

Serves 6.

LEG OF VEAL LARDED WITH HAM

Make lengthwise incisions in *a piece of veal weighing about 1 kg (2 lb)* — through the centre, then above and below — and insert strips of ham into the incisions, using *250 g (8 oz) raw ham*.

Cut *2 carrots* into strips and insert here and there.

Tie the meat securely with string, brown in a pan with *60 g (2 oz) butter* and *1 tablespoon olive oil*. Add *2 sage leaves* and pour over *1 tumblerful white wine*.

Cover and cook gently on top of the stove for 2½ hours.

To serve, cut into slices and pour the sauce over.

Serves 4.

LAUDER AND HOWARD ANTIQUES

Les Lauder's interest in antiques goes back many years. He established his business in Fremantle in 1972 and opened the present George Street premises in 1979.

The building has an interesting history. It was built in 1901 as the W.A. Brushware Factory. That business was begun in 1896 by Herbert Albrecht with just one assistant. By the time his factory opened he was employing eighteen people. His brushware won medals in Australia and Europe!

W.A. Brushware later became the Swan Brushworks, and the firm still operates from another site.

Les Lauder's love of antiques carries over to an affection for old buildings. When he settled in Fremantle his distress at seeing places being torn down caused him to initiate a public meeting to see if locals were concerned with preservation. The response was quite a shock! Over four hundred people turned up and so was established the Fremantle Society with Les Lauder as president.

It is through the efforts of the Society that more buildings in Fremantle have been given National Trust Classification than in any other area in Australia.

AMERICAN PUMPKIN PIE

This dish was made for General Douglas MacArthur when he was in Australia during the Second World War. He said he hadn't had pumpkin pie for such a long time . . . !

In a bowl put:
1 cup mashed moist pumpkin
2 eggs, beaten
¼ cup brown sugar
½ cup white sugar
½ teaspoon salt   } combined
1 tablespoon cornflour
1 teaspoon cinnamon
1 teaspoon nutmeg

Add *juice and rind of 2 lemons* and pour into a *shortcrust or biscuit pastry shell.* Bake slowly 150°C (300°F) for 45 minutes or until set.

When cool top with *whipped cream*, a sprinkle of *cinnamon* and slivers of *blanched almonds*.

* F·R·E·M·A·N·T·L·E F·O·L·K *

This section looks at some of the people of Fremantle, tells of their contributions to the city, and offers some of their favourite recipes.

ST PATRICK'S CATHOLIC CHURCH

Considered an important part of Australia's heritage, St Patrick's held its first service in 1900 — four years after the laying of the foundation stone.

This fine example of Gothic architecture was planned by the Oblate Fathers who came to Fremantle from Ireland in 1894 to develop St Patrick's Catholic parish. The leader of the Oblate Fathers was the Reverend Tom Ryan and he is credited with initiating the construction of a new church.

The original parish church had served the colony for forty years and had become far too small to accommodate the increasing population.

Even though St Patrick's operated from 1900, it was not until 1959 that the church was completed! The original design included a sanctuary, the addition of which was initiated by the efforts of the Reverend Father Sullivan.

The architect for St Patrick's was Michael Cavanagh, a member of the Western Australian Institute of Architects who designed several buildings in Fremantle and Perth.

The walls of the church are built of limestone from Cottesloe and North Fremantle, the doorways, columns, tracery windows and other architectural features are in Sydney freestone, the altar is of white marble and the pews of Western Australian jarrah.

St Patrick's most recent renovation was funded by the Bond family for their daughter's wedding in 1985.

On the eve of the nuptials the *West Australian* reported:

> Eileen Bond, proud mother of the bride, has spruced up Fremantle's 84-year-old St Patrick's Church for her daughter Suzanne's wedding tomorrow.
>
> Mrs Bond has had the altar repainted and has recarpeted the confessional and aisles.

Eileen Bond's grandparents attended the church early in the century and two stained glass windows in the church perpetuate their memory. Her parents were married at St Patrick's in 1926.

EILEEN BOND'S VICHYSSOISE

It was Alan Bond's *Australia II* success in winning the America's Cup in 1983 that made Fremantle an object of world attention. Bond's success was the 25th attempt to wrench the Auld Mug from the New York Yacht Club.

In a saucepan fry in *60 g (2 oz) butter*:
1 large onion, sliced
5 leeks, sliced
When golden brown add:
6 cups chicken stock
6 medium potatoes, peeled and chopped
Bring to boil and simmer about 45 minutes.
Cool and put the lot through a blender.
Pour back into the saucepan and add:
2 cups milk
¾ cup cream
Bring to the boil, cool, and when cold stir in an extra *¾ cup cream*. Refrigerate.
Serve hot or cold with chopped *chives*.
Serves 8.

BARBECUED SPARE RIBS

Mix:
185 g (6 oz) brown sugar
½ tablespoon celery seed
½ tablespoon salt
1 tablespoon chili powder
1 teaspoon paprika
Rub part of the mixture into *1 kg (2 lb) pork spare ribs*, and combine the rest with:
½ cup vinegar
8 tablespoons tomato sauce
½ tablespoon Worcestershire sauce
dash of Tabasco
Use this to baste. Let the ribs stand a couple of hours before barbecuing, basting all the time.
Serves 4–6.

The Oldham Family

Five generations of the Oldham family have contributed to the history of Fremantle.

For the sixteen years up to 1902, the Chief Harbour-Master, Captain C. R. T. Russell, RN, lived with his wife and family in the Harbour-Master's residence just south of the Round House. The two-storey stone building had been completed for his arrival by the Colonial Architect, George Temple-Poole. It stood on about an acre of land surrounded by garden which was protected by a high stone wall.

The building had additions made to it in 1896 when the Russells were joined by their younger daughters who had completed an education in Europe, and their son, Robert, who had come down on furlough from India, bringing a friend with him.

Like most officers of the Royal Navy at that time, Captain Russell had been trained as a competent painter in watercolours and oil. He painted many scenes in the vicinity, and several examples of his work remained in Western Australia after he returned to England in 1904 following his retirement.

Not all of the Russell family returned to England. Daughter Susan chose to remain in Australia to marry a young architect from Victoria, Charles Lancelot Oldham. Charles was responsible for many of the fine buildings and interesting precincts in the area, including the Fremantle Markets, the P&O Building in Phillimore Street (originally the Australian Steamship Company), the Marmion Memorial's Saxon Cross by the Proclamation Tree, the Esplanade Hotel and many offices, warehouses, shops and private residences in the city and its surrounding district.

Their eldest son, John B. R. Oldham, was Government Landscape Architect from 1956 to 1972. His wife, Ray, through her involvement in the Royal W.A. Historical Society, played an important role in the selection of Fremantle for the first-ever conducted inspection of the state's historical buildings. This took place in 1960 and regular tours have been organised by the R.W.A.H.S. ever since — they are now included as an important part of government and commercial tourist activities in the area.

Ray served as president of the R.W.A.H.S. from 1983 up to 1986.

John's and Ray's eldest daughter, Tish Phillips, has illustrated a book with her delightful line drawings of Fremantle buildings, and does portraits at the Fremantle Markets. She is a film-maker, working often in the area.

Second daughter Jan, journalist and gourmet cookery-writer, has written many articles on the contemporary scene and of the plans for the future of this attractive port. She is the author of two cookbooks and regularly contributes to the lifestyle pages of our national magazines and newspapers.

A great-grandson of Charles Lancelot Oldham, John Morris Oldham, is an artist of note, and a fifth generation Oldham, Jodi Oldham-Phillips is a student and designer of fabrics and fashion at the Bannister Street Workshops.

The following recipes were contributed by members of the Oldham family.

SEAFOOD BROCHETTES

Thread skewers with alternating pieces of these ingredients:
375 g (12 oz) green prawns, peeled
375 g (12 oz) scallops
1 can mangos, drained and chopped (or 1 fresh mango)
2 tomatoes, cut in chunks
1 can lychees, drained and brushed with lemon juice
or
2 fresh pears, cut into chunks and brushed with lemon juice.

Grill the skewers over hot coals and brush with this butter mixture as they cook.

Combine:
2 tablespoons melted butter
1 tablespoon soy sauce
2 teaspoons grated fresh ginger
a few tablespoons lychee liquid

Cook until prawns just turn pink. Fresh or dried garden herbs, e.g. marjoram and thyme, thrown on the coals during cooking give a lovely flavour.

Serves 6 as a main course.

WHOLE BAKED FISH

You'll need *1 large fish, about 3 kg (6 lb)*, scaled and gutted. A snapper is ideal. With a sharp knife, slash through the skin right down the bone and cut in a diamond pattern. This not only gives a decorative finish but it also helps it to cook evenly.

Mix *2 tablespoons oil* and *juice and rind of 2 lemons* and rub into the slashes.

Now fill the cavity with this *stuffing*:
In a frying pan melt *3 tablespoons butter* and fry:
4 spring onion, chopped
1 red capsicum, chopped
2 cloves garlic, finely chopped
When the spring onion is softened, remove everything from the pan and tip into a large mixing bowl.

Add:
1 cup cooked brown rice
1 tablespoon green peppercorns, crushed
juice and rind of 1 lemon
2 tablespoons butter, chopped
salt and *pepper* to taste

Sew up the cavity or secure with a long skewer.

Lift the fish onto a well-greased baking dish, leaving it upright and curling around the dish so it fits snugly.

Wrap pieces of greased foil around the fins and tail to prevent them burning during cooking.

Pour over *1 cup white wine* and *4 tablespoons butter*, melted, and bake in a moderate oven 180°C (350°F) for 45 minutes or till the flesh flakes easily with a fork — it should come easily away from the backbone.

Lift carefully onto a serving platter.

Prepare the *sauce*:
In a small saucepan mix *1 teaspoon cornflour* with *2 tablespoons cold water* and add *a few tablespoons cooking juices*. Add this mixture to the pan and bring to the boil.

Remove from the heat and stir in *2–3 tablespoons sour cream*. Bring back to boiling point but do not let it boil.

Spoon a little sauce over the fish and serve the rest separately.

This is great served with chopped *walnuts*.

Serves 6–8.

William (Cookie) Mitchell

A self-confessed larrikin, 'Cookie' Mitchell came to Fremantle from West Perth in 1942, and is well known around town for his good humour. At 72 he still has a twinkle in his eye and 'is partial to the occasional beer at the pub'. The Fremantle Hotel is his favourite haunt.

His nickname comes from short-lived employment as a pastry-cook when he was limited to putting the crosses on hot cross buns!

While Cookie admits to being something of a vagrant during the Depression years ('I used to jump trains and go from town to town looking for work, as it was really scarce') he was to spend 28 years in the Co-operative Bulk Handling Depot in North Fremantle.

However, he regards those earlier lean years as being most interesting. He enjoyed working in different places — particularly in a brewery operating a 'crowning' machine which put the lids on beer bottles.

Cookie Mitchell loves Fremantle and regards it as the friendliest place in the world.

1942

On February 18, the first convoy of United States troops called at Fremantle — The escorting warship was the U.S.N. Cruiser *Phoenix*, and the Aircraft Carrier *Langley* arrived to load fighter aircraft which had been flown across Australia and were brought by road to Victoria Quay.

Following the fall of Singapore, vessels crowded with refugees arrived at Fremantle. The harbour accommodation was severely taxed, and frequently there were as many as thirty ships at anchor in Gage Roads.

Rear Admiral Lockwood, Commander of the United States Naval Forces in Western Australia, arrived towards the end of the year to organise the submarine base, the vessels of which were to play such a decisive part in attack upon Japanese merchant shipping and vessels of war. During 1942, and in the years that followed, Fremantle Harbour was used extensively for the repair of merchant vessels damaged through enemy action, or, for other reasons, in need of overhaul.

The Western Gateway
John K. Ewers

Michael Kailis

Michael Kailis's association with Fremantle dates back to 1910 when his father George settled in the town after buying a fish shop. His mother was a former pupil of the now closed Princess May Girls' School.

With little formal schooling behind him as a child, Michael Kailis studied for his matriculation at night school while holding down a daytime job with Mobil Oil. He later studied for a diploma in mine management in Broken Hill. Returning to Perth for his sister's wedding, he was inspired with ideas for improving the lobster industry and so commenced an active involvement in the fishing industry. He began work with a relative, Theo Kailis, and adopted a new method of processing lobsters, removing the tails in such a way that more meat was retained, so increasing the yield and therefore the price.

Michael moved to Dongera in 1961. There he set up a thriving crayfish processing business, literally starting from scratch, camping at first, until the business grew. When his family joined him their accommodation was very basic and his wife, Patricia, found the facilities and fresh foodstuffs practically non-existent! With the exception of a plentiful supply of seafood that situation prevailed for some years.

Dongera in 1961 had only a few boats and a few townsfolk but Michael soon organised a fishermen's association, which is now part of the statewide Professional Fishermen's Association.

In 1963 he pioneered the prawning industry at Exmouth Gulf. The family divided time between the two places, spending summer in Dongera for the crayfish season, and the winter in Exmouth for the prawn season. Housing facilities varied — one year being spent in a Nissan hut.

To start the business in Exmouth, Michael salvaged everything he could from WA Petroleum. There was little there but a lighthouse, two stations and one airstrip at Carnarvon — no wireless and no telephone. Only twice-weekly visits by a DC3 broke the family's isolation.

The family then moved to similar conditions in Learmonth. It was here that Michael started designing prawn trawlers suitable for the area's weather conditions. The first two were built by a contractor, but when Michael befriended an old Glasgow-born shipbuilder, his company built its own trawlers. Completing 98 boats in all, he exported many to other countries, including Burma, Indonesia, Nigeria and India. The M. G. Kailis Co. was the first to build steel trawlers in Fremantle's Fisherman's Harbour.

In recent years, Michael Kailis was awarded the CBE for services to the Greek community and the fishing industry.

His advice to aspiring young business people attempting to follow in his footsteps: 'pure hard work'. His wife, Dr Patricia Kailis's advice, equally respected: 'Have a go'.

PARTY OCTOPUS

A party favourite and real talking point! *Snap-frozen octopus* are the best to use — defrosted, massaged and cleaned to remove skin.

In a frypan with hot *oil* just covering the base put *1 large onion* in the centre and sit the octopus on top — the body on the onion and the tentacles arranged around.

Add:
1 bayleaf
4 cloves
pinch cayenne pepper
1 cup rose wine

Put the lid on and simmer slowly for 20 minutes until tender (liquid should be reduced to a sauce consistency). Transfer the octopus to a serving dish, pour the sauce over and let cool to room temperature.

Put on the table with a large carving knife and let guests help themselves. This may be served as an entree or as a buffet dish. If there's any left over, cut into pieces, put in a screwtop jar and it will keep well in the refrigerator for 2–3 weeks.

Serves 16 as an entree.

SEAFOOD SAUCE

This 'special' was devised during the Kailis family's years in Learmonth when weekly supplies were the norm — no fresh foods flown in, just cans and bottles. In fact in those days it was impossible to get fresh milk or cream! Nevertheless, there was a ready abundance of fresh seafood — oysters, lobsters, prawns and bugs — and this sauce went well with all of them.

Combine in a screw-top jar:
1 can evaporated milk
equivalent amount tomato sauce
1 teaspoon horseradish sauce
dash of Worcestershire sauce

PRAWNS A LA GREQUE

This is delicious served hot or cold.
In a flameproof casserole with a little heated oil saute until soft:
2 large onions, chopped
2 cloves garlic, finely chopped

Add:
2 kg (4 lb) prawn flesh (snap-frozen block, defrosted)
1 kg (2 lb) tomatoes
½ cup white wine
1 bayleaf
pinch cayenne pepper
salt to taste

Mix well, top with *fetta cheese* in fairly thin slices.

Put the lid on and bake at 160°C (325°F) for 30–40 minutes, just until prawns are opaque.

Remove lid, cool slightly and serve with crusty *white bread, black olives* and crisp *green salad*.

Serves 16 for buffet meal.

South Beach Bathing Regulations
Male Swimming Area — Two chains South of By-the-Sea (Jenkin) Street [sic] to Two chains North of Douro Road. Female Swimming Area — Two chains North of By-the-Sea Road to Louisa Street.
                                        The Umpire, 4 February 1899

SIX AINSLIE STREET, NORTH FREMANTLE

During a drive around the city's outer area I sighted this beautiful house and without further investigation decided it must be included in this book! Fortunately its owners agreed and gave me an interesting insight into its history.

When Mr and Mrs Heaney bought the old house in 1968 it was sadly run down. After much effort, it has been restored to its original beauty.

Built in 1895 by a Mr Scanlon, its walls are made from indigenous limestone, probably quarried on site. Because this local stone is comparatively soft it was stabilised with brick quoins.

In those days the site offered magnificent views up the Swan River; today, sadly, much of the view is obstructed by unattractive buildings.

The second occupant of the house was James Leysham. He purchased it in 1919 on his return from wartime France where he had served with the 44th Battalion. When he died of an ulcer in 1930, his aunt, Mabel Ryan, took over the house and she remained there until her niece, Val Heaney, and her husband purchased it.

With a husband at sea and children away at school, Mrs Heaney was often alone in the house and during the first eight months after moving in she experienced some strange happenings.

On returning from work each day, Mrs Heaney was confronted by a dreadful smell mostly confined to the main bedroom. She took little comfort in being told by her aunt that it was the spirit of her departed grandmother manifesting itself through her old possessions now installed in the house.

Covered in goose bumps and alone, Mrs Heaney would sit in a lounge chair in the evening and sing Grandma's songs to appease the spirit! The smell was always gone by morning.

Then, when her son returned home from school she told him of the problem and agreed with his suggestion that they should swap bedrooms. However, this didn't work as the smell moved too! It was only when her son agreed that the smell must be Grandma's spirit that it disappeared and to this day has not returned. Quite a story.

The house has four identical rooms each with a fireplace. A Fremantle architect has included leadlight windows to let more light in.

Extensions to the back of the house have enhanced its comfort and attractive appearance.

Mrs Heaney's love of antiques fits in well with the old house — beautiful carpets sit on highly polished wood floors, and the leadlight front door bearing the name 'Montana' comes from some unknown estate of years gone by.

BOILED FRUITCAKE

A tried and true recipe from the collection of Val Heaney's mother.
In a saucepan put:
1 cup brown sugar
1 x 425 g (15 oz) can crushed pineapple (optional)
500 g (1 lb) mixed fruit
1 teaspoon mixed spice
1 teaspoon bicarbonate of soda
125 g (4 oz) butter
Bring to the boil and simmer 3 minutes.
Allow to cool and add:
1 cup self-raising flour
1 cup plain flour   } sifted together
2 well-beaten eggs

Turn into a greased and lined 20 cm (8 in) square tin with high sides and bake in a moderate oven 180°C (350°F) for 1¼ hours. Then reduce oven heat to slow and bake a further 35–40 minutes or until cooked when tested.

This is a good, reliable, economical, moist fruitcake.

Frank Tydeman

Frank Tydeman came to Westen Australia at the end of World War II and worked as a consultant on ports before joining the Fremantle Port Authority. In 1950 he was appointed General Manager of the Authority and during his fifteen years in office the port was developed mainly in line with his recommendations. It was a period of unprecedented expansion during which Fremantle became one of the most highly mechanised ports in the world.

Born in London in 1901, Mr Tydeman graduated at London University with a B.Sc. Engineering Degree. He had an impressive career in every aspect of port operations extending over 45 years.

Following his retirement, Mr Tydeman was awarded the CMG for his services to the Fremantle Port Authority.

Bruce Lee

Born in Fremantle in 1905, Bruce Lee, a Justice of the Peace and former councillor and journalist, is one of six children born to British parents who came to Australia at the outbreak of the Boer War.

At fifteen he left Fremantle Boys School to take a job as office boy in the local office of the *Daily News* — located at the bottom of the hill from High Street where his family lived.

For twelve shillings and sixpence a week Mr Lee swept the office and learnt much from watching journalists at work. For training in journalism he regarded the three years before his admission as 'absolutely invaluable'.

In those early days copies of the paper came by train from Perth and Mr Lee's duties included collecting them from the station — with a borrowed railway trolley — wheeling them to the *Daily News* office about 300 metres away, distributing them to the paper boys and bundling some on to trams for distribution to East and North Fremantle.

Mail boats came into the port once a week and the young journalist, on receipt of a call from the Signal Station, left home at 6 am, boarded a ferry to meet the ship at the harbour's entrance and conducted interviews with interesting passengers!

The former office boy became a senior editor for the Fremantle office, and as such he inaugurated a weekly Fremantle Supplement which, despite a few early setbacks, continued publication until long after Mr Lee's retirement in 1970.

Mr Lee has an impressive record of community service. He served on the City Council from 1940 to 1967 — as Deputy Mayor under Sir Frank Gibson and his successor Sir Frederick Samson. As Chairman of the Ovals, Parks and South Beach Committee, he looked after Fremantle Oval and initiated creation of new playing grounds. 'Bruce Lee Reserve' is named after him, as also is 'Lee Avenue'. He was the first Fremantle representative on the State Library Board of Western Australia — and its first chairman.

Bruce and Doris Lee celebrated their golden wedding anniversary in 1986. They have lived since their marriage in the same High Street house, which they built on a block bordering the rear of Samson House. The house gave sweeping harbour views and in the old days the Lees could see the big mail boats coming in.

They love Fremantle and have both made positive contributions to the community. Mrs Lee has the distinction of being the first official archivist for St John's Church — a position she held for nine years — and remains an active committee member.

PEANUT SPECIALS

Doris Lee has been making these for fifty years — frequently in large quantities for fund-raising fetes. They are much enjoyed by young and old.

Combine in a large bowl:
3 breakfast cups cornflakes
¾ cup shelled, unsalted peanuts

In a smaller bowl beat *3 large egg whites* with a *pinch of salt* until stiff but not dry.

Gently fold in:
¾ cup sugar
3 drops vanilla essence
3 teaspoons melted butter

Pour this mixture over the cornflakes and nuts and turn with a fork until well mixed.

With a teaspoon (and fingers) put tiny mounds on a greased oven tray.

Cook near the bottom of a moderately slow oven 160°C (325°F) for about 20 minutes or until golden brown.

Remove from tray while still scarcely warm — use a knife, and if biscuits start to stick, pop them back in the oven for a minute to warm again.

Horses at Church

Frank Bluett, livery stable proprietor, Adelaide Street, was fined one shilling and costs in Fremantle Police Court, for permitting 3 of his horses to graze in the grounds of St. John's Church at 11.15 p.m. on the night of 1st May. The Bench admonished Bluett, who turned his horses loose in the Churchyard last winter.

The Mail, 5 May 1905

Lucy Stitt

Fremantle is Lucy Stitt's birthplace and family home and she loves it — especially the city's old-fashioned character and ready availability of everything she needs.

Life for Mrs Stitt and her late husband was not always easy. Out of work for two years during the Depression years, he had just found a job when war broke out! Four years in the army followed. On his return from duty in the Middle East and the Pacific, Mr Stitt resumed his job as a tram driver and later worked as a customs officer.

Mrs Stitt loves cooking and when I arrived on her doorstep tantalising smells of freshly baked cakes wafted through the house — special treats for her grandchildren.

Following is one of her favourite recipes.

CRAYFISH MORNAY

Fish may be used as an alternative to crayfish for this dish.

Prepare this *sauce*:

In a saucepan melt *60 g (2 oz) butter*, off the heat stir in *60 g (2 oz) plain flour*, return to heat, let mixture bubble then stir in *2 cups milk* and *½ cup white wine*. Stir till boiling and cook 3 minutes.

Season with:
1 *onion, grated*
1 *teaspoon lemon juice*
⅓ *cup grated cheese*

In a buttered pie dish put:
a layer of *cooked crayfish or fish*
a layer of sauce

Top with another ⅓ *cup grated cheese*.

Brown under a griller and serve.

Serves 6.

Early Gun

Tuesday 'one o'clock gun' prematurely goes off 6 minutes early. Sensational confusion in the town.

Evening Mail, 2 July 1907

I·N·D·E·X O·F R·E·C·I·P·E·S

(and recipe contributors)

American Pumpkin Pie (Lauder and Howard Antiques), 78
Appertisers
Guacamole (Mexican Kitchen), 46
Kangaroo Tail and Pig's Head Brawn (C.W.A. Cookery Book (W. A.), 1936), 14
Salmon Mousse (Potters Workshop), 70
Smoked Salmon Mousse (Captain Fremantle Motor Lodge), 25
Apple Nut Pecan Cake (1897 Coffee House), 73
Auld Mug's West Coast Salad, The (Auld Mug Tavern), 62
Aunty Alice's Orange Bar Cake (Alice Gerrard), 13

Barbecued Spare Ribs (Eileen Bond), 81
Beef
Beef Curry (Pioneer Cafe), 33
Beef and Orange Sate (John Gordon), 75
Canterbury Crockpot Silverside (Fremantle Hotel), 51
Savoury Rissoles (Mr Pickwick's Gourmet Shop), 27
Beef Curry (Pioneer Cafe), 33
Beef and Orange Sate (John Gordon), 75
Biscuits
Peanut Specials (Doris Lee), 93
Boiled Fruitcake (Val Heaney), 91
Bread and Butter Pudding (Dorothy Connolly), 15
Bread, Home-made (Marjorie Baguley), 14

Cakes
Apple Nut Pecan Cake (1897 Coffee House), 73
Aunty Alice's Orange Bar Cake (Alice Gerrard), 13
Boiled Fruitcake (Val Heaney), 91
Lucy's Date Loaf (Lucy Stitt), 24
Pioneer Cafe Scones (Pioneer Cafe), 33
Pumpkin Fruit Cake (Fremantle Museum and Arts Centre Coffee Shop), 67
Vanilla Slices (Culley's Tea Rooms), 43
Canterbury Crockpot Silverside (Fremantle Hotel), 51
Ceviche (Mexican Kitchen), 46
Cheese and Ham Muffins (Princess Coffee Lounge), 41
Chicken
Chicken Roxanne (Auld Mug Tavern), 62
Chicken and Spaghetti (Roma Restaurant), 34
Filo Chicken (National Hotel), 56
Five Spice Apricot Drumsticks (Princess Coffee Lounge), 41

Yaki Tori (Lombardo's Fisherman's Landing), 29
Chicken Roxanne (Auld Mug Tavern), 62
Chicken and Spaghetti (Roma Restaurant), 34
Cobbler and Green Peppercorns (Oyster Beds Restaurant), 44
Crab and Pear Entree (Oyster Beds Restaurant), 45
Crayfish Martinique (Captain Fremantle Motor Lodge), 26
Crayfish Mornay (Lucy Stitt), 94
Cream of Cauliflower Soup (Timothy's Toys), 76
Cream of Garlic Prawns (Federal Hotel), 48
Cream of Walnut Soup (1897 Coffee House), 72
Curry
Beef Curry (Pioneer Cafe), 33
Squid Curry (Harper and Whittington's Spice Shop), 74

Desserts
Bread and Butter Pudding (Dorothy Connolly), 15
Frozen Banana Ice-cream (The Health Hut), 42

Eileen Bond's Vichyssoise (Eileen Bond), 81

Fettuccine con Broccoli (Papa Luigi's), 39
Fettuccine with Cheese and Bacon Sauce (Coufie's Cafe), 31
Filo Chicken (National Hotel), 56
Fish and Seafood
Ceviche (Mexican Kitchen), 46
Cobbler and Green Peppercorns (Oyster Beds Restaurant), 44
Fish Patties (Cafe 33), 36
Party Octopus (Patricia Kailis), 87
Quenelles of Snapper with Sweet Pepper Sauce (Mason's Brasserie), 58
Scampa alla Griglie (Papa Luigi's), 38
Seafood Brochettes (Tish Oldham Phillips), 83
Squid Curry (Harper and Whittington's Spice Shop), 74
Whole Baked Fish (John Oldham), 84
Fisherman's Pie (Lombardo's Fisherman's Landing), 30
Fish Patties (Cafe 33), 36
Five Spice Apricot Drumsticks (Princess Coffee Lounge), 41
Fresh Crab (Norfolk Hotel), 64
Frozen Banana Ice-cream (The Health Hut), 42

Guacamole (Mexican Kitchen), 46

INDEX * 96

Golden Pink Punch (The Health Hut), 42
Ham and Egg Quiche (Pioneer Cafe), 32
Home-made Bread (Marjorie Baguley), 14
Kangaroo Tail and Pig's Head Brawn (C.W.A. Cookery Book (W. A.), 1936), 14
Lamb Fillets on a bed of Leeks with Beaujolais Sauce (Mason's Brasserie), 59
Leg of Veal larded with Ham (Timothy Toy's), 77
Lentil and Vegetable Soup (The Health Hut), 42
Lucy's Date Loaf (Lucy Stitt), 24
Norfolk Patties (The Bread and Cheese Shop), 40
Party Octopus (Patricia Kailis), 87
Pasta
   Fettuccine con Broccoli (Papa Luigi's), 39
   Fettuccine with Cheese and Bacon Sauce (Coufie's Cafe), 31
   Pasta with Marinara Sauce (Potters Workshop), 69
   Pasta with Marinara Sauce (Potters Workshop), 69
Peanut Specials (Doris Lee), 93
Pecan Pie (Federal Hotel), 49
Pies
   American Pumpkin Pie (Lauder and Howard Antiques), 78
   Fisherman's Pie (Lombardo's Fisherman's Landing), 30
   Ham and Egg Quiche (Pioneer Cafe), 32
   Pecan Pie (Federal Hotel), 49
Pioneer Cafe Scones (Pioneer Cafe), 33
Pork
   Barbecued Spare Ribs (Eileen Bond), 81
Prawn Cutlets (National Hotel), 56
Prawns a la Greque (Patricia Kailis), 88
Pumpkin Fruit Cake (Fremantle Museum and Arts Centre Coffee Shop), 67
Pumpkin Soup (Mr Pickwick's Gourmet Shop), 27
Quenelles of Snapper with Sweet Pepper Sauce (Mason's Brasserie), 58
Rabbit Paste (C.W.A. Cookery Book (W. A.), 1936), 19
Salads
   Seafood Salad (Lido Restaurant), 37
   Spinach Salad with Bacon Dressing (1897 Coffee House), 73
   Auld Mug's West Coast Salad,The (Auld Mug Tavern), 62
Salmon Mousse (Potters Workshop), 70
Savoury Rissoles (Mr Pickwick's Gourmet Shop), 27
Scallops Feuillete (Esplanade Hotel), 51
Scaloppini con Carciofi (Papa Luigi's), 38
Scampa alla Griglie (Papa Luigi's), 38

Seafood Brochettes (Tish Oldham Phillips), 83
Seafood Salad (Lido Restaurant), (Lido Cafe), 37
Seafood Sauce (Patricia Kailis), 88
Shellfish
   Crab and Pear Entree (Oyster Beds Restaurant), 45
   Crayfish Martinique (Captain Fremantle Motor Lodge), 26
   Crayfish Mornay (Lucy Stitt), 94
   Cream of Garlic Prawns (Federal Hotel), 48
   Fresh Crab (Norfolk Hotel), 64
   Prawn Cutlets (National Hotel), 56
   Prawns a la Greque (Patricia Kailis), 88
   Scallops Feuillete (Esplanade Hotel), 51
Smoked Salmon Mousse (Captain Fremantle Motor Lodge), 25
Snacks
   Cheese and Ham Muffins (Princess Coffee Lounge), 41
   Stovies (C.W.A. Cookery Book (W. A.), 1936), 11
   Suffolk Marys (C.W.A. Cookery Book (W.A.), 1936), 11
Soup
   Cream of Cauliflower Soup (Timothy's Toys), 76
   Cream of Walnut Soup (1897 Coffee House) 72
   Eileen Bond's Vichyssoise (Eileen Bond), 81
   Lentil and Vegetable Soup (The Health Hut), 42
   Pumpkin Soup (Mr Pickwick's Gourmet Shop), 27
   Spinach, New Potato and Cheese Slice (Cafe 33), 35
   Spinach Salad with Bacon Dressing (1897 Coffee House), 73
   Squid Curry (Harper and Whittington's Spice Shop), 74
   Stovies (C.W.A. Cookery Book (W. A.), 1936), 11
   Suffolk Marys (C.W.A. Cookery Book (W. A.), 1936), 11
Vanilla Slices (Culley's Tea Rooms), 43
Veal
   Leg of Veal larded with Ham (Timothy's Toys), 77
   Scallopini con Carciofi (Papa Luigi's) 38
Vegetarian
   Norfolk Patties (The Bread and Cheese Shop), 40
   Spinach, New Potato and Cheese Slice (Cafe 33), 35
Whole Baked Fish (John Oldham), 84
Yaki Tori (Lombardo's Fisherman's Landing), 29